C0-DXA-264

R00582 28377

```
LB          Bailey, A. J.
2831.826
.G7         Support for
B35           school
1987          management
```

$31.00

DATE		

SOCIAL SCIENCES AND HISTORY DIVISION
EDUCATION & PHILOSOPHY

© THE BAKER & TAYLOR CO.

SUPPORT FOR SCHOOL MANAGEMENT

CROOM HELM EDUCATIONAL MANAGEMENT SERIES
Edited by Cyril Poster

STAFF DEVELOPMENT IN THE SECONDARY SCHOOL
Chris Day and Roger Moore

CHALLENGES IN EDUCATIONAL MANAGEMENT
W.F. Dennison and Ken Shenton

PREPARING SCHOOL LEADERS FOR EDUCATIONAL IMPROVEMENT
K.A. Leithwood, W. Rutherford and R. Van der Veght

Support for School Management

A.J. Bailey

The report of a project funded by the Department of Education and Science on the design and provision of support for headteachers and others undertaking school management training.

CROOM HELM
London • Sydney • Wolfeboro, New Hampshire

SOCIAL SCIENCE & HISTORY DIVISION
EDUCATION & PHILOSOPHY SECTION

© 1987 A.J. Bailey
Croom Helm Ltd, Provident House, Burrell Row,
Beckenham, Kent, BR3 1AT

Croom Helm Australia, 44-50 Waterloo Road,
North Ryde, 2113, New South Wales

British Library Cataloguing in Publication Data
Bailey, A.J.
   Support for school management.
   1. High schools — Great Britain —
   Administration
   I. Title
   373.12′00941   LB2822.3.G7

ISBN 0-7099-5033-0

Croom Helm, 27 South Main Street,
Wolfeboro, New Hampshire 03894-2069, USA

Library of Congress Cataloging-in-Publication Data
Bailey, A.J.
   Support for school management.

   Bibliography: p.
   1. School administrators — Training — Great Britain.
2. Continuing education — Great Britain. I. Title.
LB2831.826.G7B35   1987   371.2′00941   86-29040
ISBN 0-7099-5033-0

Printed and bound in Great Britain

CONTENTS

Acknowledgements

Introduction and Overview   1

1 Review of Current Practice   7
   Provision of Management Training for Secondary
   School Headteachers   7
   Current State of Support for Training   13

**2 A Planning Framework for Training and Support
at the Local Level**   26
   Establishing a Joint Plan   26
   The Course Design Phase   31
   Recruitment and the Process of Negotiation   35
   Support for Management Action: an Overview   39

3 Support for Personal Action   44
   The Management Self Development Workshop   44
   Mutual Support Groups   50
   Keeping a Personal Journal   56

4 Support for Corporate Action   60
   The Action Learning Set   60
   External Consultancy   70
   LEA Task Groups   72
   Cascade Training   75

**5 Developing New Forms of Training Opportunities
to promote the Transition to Better Systems of
Management Development**   84
   The Case for Incremental Change   84
   The Transition to More Effective Management
   Development   88
   The Dimension of Personal Development   90
   The Dimension of School Development   94
   The Dimension of Development External
   to the School   101

6	**Comments and Observations from the Field**	105
	Comments on the Use of Self	
	Development Activities	105
	Experiences of Keeping a Journal	116
	Reports on Action Learning Experiments	120
	Support after School Management Training	130

Conclusion and Recommendations arising from the Project 139

Annotated Bibliography: a guide to information and resources available to those planning support activities at the local level — 143

Self Development	143
Mutual Support Groups	157
Keeping a Professional Journal	161
Action Learning	163
Consultancy	170
The LEA Task Group	174

FOREWORD

The University of Sussex has long been recognised as one of the leading providers of school management training in the United Kingdom. From the outset it established and developed close links with the LEAs and the schools within the region, arguing that the effectiveness of management training can best be gauged at what Tony Bailey calls 'the point of application': the school itself.

It soon became apparent that, however close the working relationship with the schools might be, courses in management training were of limited value unless the management concepts propounded on the courses were directly relevant to the experiences and the needs of the school managers. For trainers the implications of this are considerable: there must be a continuing dialogue and partnership with the client schools and the LEAs so that courses had as their start point a clear and realistic focus on the management issues being encountered in the field.

Secondly, it was a commonplace among providers to regard the course itself as an effective agent of change. For this assumption there is little or no research evidence. The course may be the catalyst, but continuing catalytic action requires support at the point of application. How this support may best be provided is the topic of the earlier chapters of this book.

The establishment by the Department of Education and Science in April 1983 of funding for courses in a number of priority areas including school management was an important step; yet the impetus for training which it provided might well have led providers and clients alike to lose sight of other, possibly more effective forms of training. One such form of training, action learning, is becoming increasingly of interest and attractive to educationists. Later chapters of this book examine critically its application to school management and, particularly, the demands it makes upon its practitioners.

Not least among the merits of this book is the very useful annotated bibliography that relates to the support activities outlined in Chapters 4 and 5.

Cyril Poster

ACKNOWLEDGEMENTS

There are in fact many authors of this book. Each has played an important part in researching the project and writing up the findings.

First mention must be given to the three senior fellows seconded to the project. Jim Knight, Graham Morris and Jack Waddilove were responsible for almost all the fieldwork and their hand can be seen in the many reports of interviews and experimental action which run through all sections of the book. Our regular team meetings and frequent debates on management training and development were at the heart of the project.

My colleagues at Sussex, Eric Briault, Tony Becher, Michael Eraut and Heather Nicholas also made major contributions. Eric worked closely with the senior fellows in conducting interviews with local education authorities; with Michael he has given invaluable support throughout the project. Tony helped and advised on fieldwork and edited the extracts from the field report contained in Chapter Six. Heather has worked as information officer to the project, researching and compiling the annotated bibliography.

Help was also forthcoming from the National Development Centre for School Management Training, with Michael Wallace contributing the survey of existing management training and Ray Bolam offering much help and advice.

Finally, the thanks of the whole team are due to the many headteachers, officers, inspectors and management trainers who gave freely of their time and experience to help us in our work.

Tony Bailey,
University of Sussex
May 1986

INTRODUCTION AND OVERVIEW

This project grew out of our early efforts in Sussex to launch a regional school management programme. In the late seventies a small group of Sussex heads, with help from major industrial and commercial firms, experimented with several management development activities. Encouraged by this support, the group conceived the notion of a broader regional programme of short management courses, self-help study groups and surveys of good practice. The programme would be backed officially by the LEAs, supported by the University and local industry, but planned and executed by experienced heads.

The formal launching of the Sussex Regional School Management Programme coincided almost to the day with the press release announcing the national initiative in school management training. The Regional Programme, with the backing of the LEAs, developed a series of one term and twenty day courses. However, our earlier experience had convinced us that training alone was inadequate. If newly acquired ideas are to be effective, they must be taken away and worked out in practice. Individuals may be capable of conducting this process of practical integration privately, but there is a far greater chance that skills and knowledge will be used (rather than stored or displayed) if continuing support is available in or close to the point of application – the school.

Put in the context of the national initiative, the organiser of every regional programme must from the outset ask the question: what does a participant need to do before attending a major training course and what support should be available upon return?

This project was established to answer this question. The Sussex Regional School Management Programme approached the DES for support and in Autumn 1983 approval was given to fund a project based at the University of Sussex in 1984/85. Three experienced heads were seconded to form the project team with members of the School of Education. In the hope of achieving results within a short time scale we decided to concentrate on secondary school management. Here, the greatest problems are encountered in providing support for heads, since they have no immediate superior easily available to them. Consequently we focussed our enquiries on the secondary head. However, the general principles of support which we outline are applicable to all school management courses.

Aims and Organisation

Working in collaboration with LEAs and industrial management, the project team's objectives were:
- to develop and evaluate experimental activities thought to support the effective utilisation of newly acquired skills and knowledge in the management of secondary schools;
- to draw up detailed, generally applicable recommendations for regional support programmes which complement the development of management training courses and improve their effectiveness.

The outline proposal, drawn up in the early summer of 1983, envisaged small scale experiments before the first round of Sussex twenty day training programmes began in Spring 1984. Unfortunately the project could not begin until January 1984 with the three seconded headteachers working only on a part-time basis for the first two terms. In these circumstances, the Steering Committee approved a two phase programme.

In the first (part-time) phase (March to October 1984) we surveyed the kinds of support currently available to heads, locating examples of good practice which the project might draw upon in developing a framework for action. The project team planned a selective series of interviews:
- with heads, deputies and advisers to survey their perceptions of the need for support;
- with LEAs, providing institutions, course members and teacher associations to estimate the range and pattern of existing support;
- with management training establishments in the public and private sectors to draw on best practice.

The scope of the project did not permit a complete survey of practice, nor was it possible to consult all LEAs or providing institutions. Our brief was to consult on a selective basis, using peer group recommendations to establish an appropriate range of contacts. In this, we are indebted to the National Development Centre for School Management Training and to HMI. The Institute of Manpower Studies gave valuable advice on contacts outside education.

We also contacted course directors, LEA officers and headteachers preparing to undertake management training or who had recently completed it, to seek their assistance in assessing the usefulness of various support activities. The intention was to work mainly with the group of authorities collaborating with the University of Sussex in the provision of management training; but two other working contacts were established, with the Somerset LEA and with the North West Educational Management Centre.

In the second phase (Autumn 1984 to Autumn 1985) we monitored good practice which the surveys had located and collaborated with local groups in planning and developing support. This provided the basis for our recommendations for support for the management training experience.

In maintaining this schedule we encountered difficulties, not least the effect of industrial action in the schools. Throughout the life of the project, heads have had to weigh carefully their commitment to external activities. Understandably, this has caused many of them to reduce preparation and follow-up activities and has discouraged course directors and LEA officers from attempting ambitious programmes of support. Consequently our arrangements for collaborative development required some adjustment. We found it necessary to limit the involvement of individual heads to quite small pieces of experimentation. Thus, for example, separate groups were established to experiment with briefing sessions, diary and journal exercises, mutual support seminars and management self-development workshops.

Towards the end of the project, in September 1985, we brought together the various elements into a composite regional planning framework for trial and implementation with the LEAs engaging in the Sussex programme.

Management Training and Management Development

Our main purpose is to make detailed recommendations on activities designed to provide support for the school management training experience. This we do and detailed accounts of activities form the bulk of the report. However, such detailed recommendations need to be located within a broader framework of local policy and here there are choices to be made.

There is a growing body of opinion which regards the establishment of comprehensive programmes of management development at LEA level as a first requirement: effective management development involves a range of activities, on and off the job, to assess personal development needs in the context of the authority's educational policies and programmes; training programmes are but one part of these activities and doubt is cast on their practical value in the absence of any systematic appraisal of personal and institutional development needs. We subscribe to this broader definition of management development and the role of training within it. However, in our opinion, there is scope for several short and medium term developments in training which will maintain the momentum established by the first two years of the national initiative in moving towards the long term goal.

The National Development Centre for School Management Training (NDC) has responded to the call for management development systems by establishing a pilot scheme with LEAs which is attempting to produce appropriate models and procedures. However, not all LEAs will be ready to adopt such a major change at this stage and would encounter difficulties in moving quickly to implement a comprehensive and effective programme. The NDC itself has already indicated the need for a careful and deliberate transition to comprehensive systems of management development.

This report complements the work of the NDC by examining the range of intermediate actions available to LEAs in moving to the position where fully fledged management development programmes are feasible:
- support for school management should be developed incrementally over the next few years towards effective management development programmes.

The argument for a policy of incremental change is strengthened when placed in the perspective of developments over the past five years. There are good grounds for assuming that we are in transition from the 'patchy and uneven provision' observed by the Hughes Report (1981) towards the management development programmes envisaged by the NDC; but it would be a mistake to assume that the transition is completed. The general increase in the level of awareness of management development issues, engendered by the national initiative, needs to be consolidated and developed further. The task of the moment is to accelerate this trend and to point it in the right direction.

However, in determining what that direction should be, it is important to recognise that the national initiative has created a changing situation with local education authorities at various stages of development. Our limited enquiries revealed that a few authorities are already embarking on radical experiments designed to move them on towards integrated and comprehensive programmes of management development. However, for most authorities the priority remains to consolidate their planning procedures in association with providing institutions, both for course design and for providing the support which participating heads need after the course. In all authorities the pressure upon the advisory and support services has increased in recent years and the resource available to help heads make good use of training is very limited. It is especially important therefore that the available resource is effectively deployed through well laid plans.

Put simply, there are two kinds of 'best practice'. Each authority must determine its own balance of effort between consolidating existing provision and experimenting with new patterns of management training and development. The need to consolidate and the need to experiment are not mutually exclusive options. The distinction is that consolidation is an immediate need for all, whilst experimental development is a desirable medium term strategy, with the timing varying from one authority to another.

Consequently, we recommend the adoption of a two-stage strategy of incremental development at the local level:

immediate action to make the best use of current training provision by consolidating arrangements for effective briefing of participants and the provision of support for subsequent action in the schools (see Chapters Two, Three and Four);

a medium term policy of experimentation with different forms of training provision designed to connect training more directly to the issues and problems of school management which the heads encounter and in some cases to incorporate management action and management change within the training experience (see Chapter Five).

Together, these two steps will give school management and LEA officers valuable experience of the kinds of working relationships, discussions and coordinated planning which are the essence of management development. They will prepare the ground for more systematic developments.

The Structure of the Report

We are very conscious that our main brief concerns only the first part of this two-stage strategy: the need to consolidate support for management training. This remains our principal concern, but informed opinion from many sources, including management trainers from the public and the private sectors, directed us towards the need for experiment in course design. In furthering our understanding of the basic relationship between management training and management development, we found it necessary to consider some of the options available. We decided that we could not fulfil our brief adequately without extending this report to include at least one chapter setting out the case for experimental development at the local level and the contribution it can make to the transition to comprehensive systems of management development.

After a short review in Chapter One of current practice the next three chapters are concerned with the immediate action required to consolidate current arrangements. Essentially we propose the establishment of a 'Joint Plan' by the various partners collaborating at the local level. The Joint Plan would include the arrangements for providing both the training and the support needed to ensure that it can be put to good practical use in the school. We indicate the types of supporting activities before, during and after training, which might be included in the Joint Plan, giving sufficient detail for an informed choice to be made and plans laid for implementation.

In Chapter Five we present the case for local experiments in training. We consider the case for changes in mid-career management education which would place greater emphasis on experiential learning and on real (as opposed to simulated) issues of educational management. We offer examples of training directed towards personal development, school development and the development of co-ordinated action at the local level.

Finally we feel it is important to pass on some of the personal experiences which were made available to us through our survey of current practice in both public and private sector training. Chapter Six offers a selection of extracts and summaries from our field reports on the experiences encountered in management training and development by heads and others.

Reference

HUGHES, M CARTER, J & FIDLER, B 1981 *Professional development provision for senior staff in schools and colleges* University of Birmingham, Department of Social and Administrative Studies in Education.

CHAPTER ONE
Review of Current Practice

Our brief is to suggest ways of helping heads make good practical use of their management training and our efforts have been concentrated on a search for methods of support. To a large extent we have been dependent on the help and advice of those engaged in the provision of management training, in industry and commerce as well as in education. Accordingly, our contacts with management trainers were designed essentially as a search for good practice rather than a balanced survey of the field. Nevertheless, we must set our recommendations in context.

This chapter is divided into two parts. The first is a review of current school management training provision as represented by the course submissions seen by the National Centre for School Management Training and Development (NDC). We are indebted to Mr. Mike Wallace of NDC for this review. The second part represents our own assessment of the current state of support for the training experience in terms of preparation and follow-up activities.

In writing this chapter, both we and the NDC are aware that our information is partial and that, in any case, practice is changing rapidly under the national initiative. Even as we conducted the project there was a noticeable move towards more experiential learning, and a greater sense of responsibility for the outcomes of training. We incorporate some of this in Chapter Five. However our review in this chapter relates to the situation as we found it in 1984 and early 1985 and although many will have made improvements in their arrangements since then, this provides a baseline for our recommendations.

Part One: Provision of Management Training for Secondary School Headteachers

This survey is based upon those course proposals and evaluation reports that have been made available to the NDC for the school year 1984/5, and upon reports of visits to courses made by Centre staff; the source of information is not, therefore, comprehensive, particularly as a number of proposals make provision for participants to negotiate and modify parts of the programme. Moreover, the overview presented here is only concerned with those courses which are open to secondary heads and does not reflect the full picture of training for headteachers or senior staff in primary schools.

In 1984/5 some 171 secondary heads received management training through 28 programmes provided by 21 specialised institutions or consortia in England (table 1). The great majority of LEAs took advantage of the special funding arrangements outlined in DES Circular 4/84; forty supported management training for the secondary heads covered in this survey. The proportion of female to male attenders (about 1:5) broadly reflects the ratio of female to male secondary heads in post (approximately 1:6).

Training provision consists of basic (twenty day minimum) courses intended to improve the managerial performance of participants in their own schools, and 'one term training opportunities' (OTTO) programmes and fellowships, the declared aim of which was to train participants as trainers of their colleagues in other schools. OTTO programmes have ranged over courses with a high component of individually negotiated learning, through 'training of the trainers' courses, to extended basic courses. This analysis covers only that component of training designed to relate to participants' performance as managers; it does not relate to wider aspects of staff development in the school.

Table 1: Summary of Provision 1984/85

Types of Training Provision	BASIC (minimum 20 days)	OTTO (One Term Training Opportunity)	Totals
No. of attenders: Female	19	10	29
Male	61	61	122
Total attendance			151
No. providing institutions or consortia involved	13	11	
No. of courses:			
For secondary heads only	6	6	
For secondary heads and senior staff	7	4	
For secondary heads and primary staff	0	1	
For secondary and primary heads and senior staff	1	3	

Practical Aims of Training

Broadly speaking, the stated aims of all the proposals for training included the intention to help improve participants' managerial performance in their schools, an improvement which ultimately can only be judged in terms of its effect on the quality of educational experience offered to pupils. In consequence, this intention to improve managerial performance in post presupposes sustained action in school after and possibly during a course. Responsibility for this lies outside the formal remit of trainers, though some extended their support as part of the training experience.

Within a course, training activities took place in one or more of three types of situation:
- in a setting both institutionally different and geographically separated from participants' schools;
- within participants' or other schools but not directly related to participants' own performance in post;
- in participants' schools, as part of their managerial performance as headteachers.

The national training initiative, with its special funds for teacher replacement and pooling arrangements for courses organised by specialist institutions, has been successful in imparting a far greater sense of urgency to the provision of practically orientated school management training. However, the effectiveness of these arrangements has to some extent been responsible for a bias of provision towards the first of these categories. The situation is summarised in Table 2 which gives some indication of the dominance of 'away from the job' training.

Preparation

Pre-course preparation arrangements showed some variation: in the majority of cases participants appear to have been expected to undertake nothing more than some general reading. Two providing institutions are on record as having organised one or more pre-course briefing sessions where aims and expectations might be clarified; in addition, tutors from one institution visited each participant in school before the course began.

Approaches to Training

Activities addressed a range of management topics whose content showed some variation between courses, tending to focus upon major task areas such as management of the curriculum, staff, external relations or change. Variation often related to particular client groups: one course was aimed at newly appointed heads, another was for heads of community schools, for example. Only one course outlined its content in terms of areas of personal skill.

It is recognised that course designers hold various assumptions about the process of adult mid-career learning and development based within a temporary system. These may be expressed in such terms as a learning cycle and individual learning styles (Kolb and Fry 1975), technical and practical knowledge (Oakeshott 1967) or matching individuals' 'theories of action' with 'theories in use' displayed in practice (Argyris and Schon 1974). However, it is convenient here to summarise the provision made in terms of three heuristic categories:

- opportunities for participants to raise their awareness of management issues and approaches;
- opportunities to acquire new management tools, techniques and skills;
- opportunities to address directly some of the management problems encountered by participants in their schools.

Table 2: Number of Courses Offering Opportunities in Various Situations 1984/85

		Training Situation		
		Away from the job	Close to the job	On the job
Type of Opportunity	Raising Awareness	28	11	8
	Skills Training	6	2	0
	Problem Solving	8	1	11

Awareness Raising

By far the largest area of provision was in raising awareness in situations away from participants' jobs. All courses aimed to heighten awareness, often making considerable use of lectures, videos, case studies and opportunities for reading, by visits to management situations outside education and through individual projects related to participants' own schools. While aiming to introduce attenders to ideas and situations outside their previous experience, most courses stressed the importance of participants' practical experience as a platform for learning. 'Experiential learning' was used in course proposals either to indicate learning about the experience of others and drawing upon one's own experience, or learning through direct experience. Thus participants were encouraged to contribute their past experience through discussion groups or by leading seminars. Learning through direct experience occurred in simulations and role-play activities. Direct experience was therefore vicarious in the sense of being direct experience of a training activity, not – by definition – of the real job situation. One course aimed to establish a network between participants, past course members, LEA advisers and course tutors to prepare the way for informal peer support after the course was over.

Visits to participants' and other schools was the most common activity designed to raise awareness in a situation closer to participants' jobs: in one case course members – newly appointed heads – shadowed an experienced colleague in his or her school; in a second, participants undertook an investigation into a management issue in another school.

On-the-job activities were uncommon; in eight instances participants were supported in reviewing some aspect of the management of their schools through individual projects where action, sometimes including other members of staff, was taken to raise awareness of the management issue. In most cases course members drew up an action plan as part of the course but not necessarily with any firm expectation of managerial action in the light of the review.

Skills Training

Most courses aimed to enhance the managerial skills of participants so that their performance in school would improve. The majority of courses raised awareness of managerial skills; but participants learned about skills, with less emphasis on practising them. In six courses participants practised specific skills, including counselling, assertiveness and decision-making, within the context of the providing institution; in others, skills were practised less directly through role-play. In one case course members received training in interpersonal skills at the training centre of a large company.

'Close to the job' skill training was confined largely to raising awareness through structured observation schedules or practice in research fieldwork skills. There were no instances of support, as part of a course, for specific training in managerial skills in post except insofar as awareness was raised and, occasionally, practice given away from the job.

Problem-solving

While all participants were given opportunities to raise their awareness of problems connected with their job as headteachers through structured or informal discussions, few addressed these problems directly as part of a course in the sense of taking any action related specifically to implementing solutions to the problems. In one case participants made a 'contract', agreeing to implement a change in their schools after the course.

Of the eight courses where opportunities were given for job related problem-solving, six confined activities within the course to planning action to be taken afterwards. The single instance of a problem solving activity taking place close to the job consisted of investigations reviewing a management issue in another participant's school.

As mentioned earlier, most of the courses purporting to offer 'action learning' or problem-solving opportunities in participants' own schools actually supported some process of review, leaving subsequent managerial action to be taken outside the context of the course. On one course participants reviewed a management problem and made a presentation to fellow participants from other schools, outlining action planned in the light of the review. In only a single case did the majority of participants take managerial action subsequent to a review, as an integral part of the course. However, three of the proposals for 1985/86 relating to courses for secondary heads received so far by the NDC indicate the intention of course organisers to include in the course the opportunity for managerial action in school. Of the evaluation reports received to date by the

NDC, none addresses directly the issue of whether participants have actually attempted to improve their performance in taking any form of managerial action during or after the course. Thus there is little evidence of the effectiveness of training.

Follow-up

There is a widespread assumption that raising participants' awareness, discussing or giving practice in management skills away from the job, or supporting a review of an issue related to individuals' jobs will lead to improvement in managerial performance. Under the special regulations, providing institutions are not vested with any reponsibility for supporting follow-up. Follow-up activities organised by tutors as part of courses or at the request of participants usually consisted of one or two meetings at the providing institution. In one case an informal network has been established and, in another, tutors are visiting each participant in his or her school several months after completion of the course.

Part Two: The Current State of Support for Training

We approach this question of support for training from three sources. First we draw on our survey of current practice amongst local education authorities. Second we examine the support offered by the providing institutions. Finally we include the findings of our discussions with a number of management trainers outside education. This forms the basis of our recommendations for immediate action set out in Chapters Two, Three and Four.

Local Education Authority Policies and Programmes

Our investigation of the developing role of the local education authorities in providing support for secondary heads undergoing management training has gone through three stages. To begin with, the research project grew out of the programme of activities at the University of Sussex. Consequently, our first stage of enquiry focussed on the four counties associated with the Sussex secondary school management programme. At a second stage we decided to enquire into the support provided by a few urban authorities known to have strong inspector/adviser teams. Our third stage was to seek information from other authorities chosen on the advice of HMI and the National Development Centre for School Management Training.

Already, before the national initiative was launched, the education authorities with whom we have been in touch were offering a combination of management training provided by the authority itself and support for individuals attending courses provided by other bodies, both educational and industrial. However, the range of opportunities presently provided varies quite sharply.

There is in one county, for example, a bare minimum of a one-day induction for new heads (effectively a know-how visit to County Hall), a termly one-day meeting of heads with the CEO and other officers and some part-time after school courses at teachers' centres. The initiative on enrolment on more substantial courses seems to come, as far as secondary schools are concerned, from the individual: the role of the authority, via the advisory service, is to approve the attendance and expenditure. Since these courses are largely for personal development rather than corporate action within the school, post-course support is limited to conversational interest on the part of the pastoral or secondary school adviser/inspector. In another LEA, the in-house provision is weightier: a two-day induction course, four-day courses for deputy heads and an annual three to four-day residential course for all secondary heads. All these are essentially know-how courses, addressing current problems and developments. The pastoral inspectors are little involved. At the other end of the spectrum we find the Inner London Education Authority, with a long-standing series of management training arrangements provided largely by the inspectorate, taking the form at present of six-week courses for secondary heads invited on a selective basis but intended eventually to cover all or most heads. Recruitment is determined through discussions amongst inspectors and with heads to produce agreed nominations. However, arrangements for follow-up activities appear to depend upon separate initiatives taken by divisional inspectors. Surrey, over a period of eight years, offered management training to every one of its secondary heads. This training took the form of a course run by the county inspectorate and extending over a full school year. A residential session was followed by a meeting each month in a member's school. The inspectorate had a clear recruitment policy, making deliberate efforts to balance course membership each year to provide a mix of new and experienced heads. Preparation focussed upon self-analysis intended to identify personal and institutional needs. An important aspect of the follow-up to the course involved each head in drawing up an institutional development plan to open up curriculum aspirations and to relate staff training opportunities to the needs which these plans indicate. The development plan was negotiated with the Chief Inspector.

In looking at the use made of longer external courses by authorities, including the first one term (OTTO) and twenty day basic courses, we have been interested to learn about selection for the courses, pre-course preparation and post-course action. The new initiatives necessarily involved authorities more with the course providers than in the past and again we find a spectrum of authority behaviour. At one end of the spectrum there is very limited involvement, perhaps no more than a 'phone call and a letter of nomination. At the other, there is more detailed consultation such as that associated, for example, with the consortium arrangements set up in Yorkshire and Humberside.

There is great variety of behaviour among authorities in the selection of people to attend longer courses on which the authority has decided to take up places. One county issued an open invitation to apply to all its 143 secondary heads and selected ten for an OTTO course and fifteen for a basic course from applicants. The former appear to have been chosen as likely to become especially useful to the authority's plans for future management training programmes, the latter as being neither new heads nor 'veterans'. In other authorities heads are nominated with little consultation and some feel that they have been 'told to go', sometimes at short notice, and wonder why. Some post-course comments from participants included the following:

- "I only had two weeks' notice ... so there was no time for any consultation about my topic".
- "I was told I was to be nominated so I asked what I'd done wrong".
- "I'd had an idea which I'd discussed with my adviser who suggested I came on this".
- "I came on this because of a chance conversation with the senior adviser".

In these circumstances, pre-course preparation tends to be left to the initiative of the provider, who may attempt to involve an authority adviser or simply make direct contact with nominated heads. The contribution of providing institutions is considered in the next section of this chapter.

When we tried to find out about post-course support, we found it difficult to distinguish between the support generally available to heads on management issues and support specifically related to course attendance. Where an authority has advisers each with a general or pastoral responsibility for a limited number of secondary schools, the adviser is likely to 'have a chat' with the head after the course. In a number of the authorities we looked at, the advisers are too few and too hard pressed to do more than respond to urgent appeals for help. In many authorities, advisers have specific subject responsibilities and pastoral care of a number of schools is additional to what is often still regarded as their main task. At these early stages of developing systematic training programmes, there is little evidence of specific follow-up on the initiative of the authority.

Spontaneous networking arising from the course is another matter. In ILEA, the pastoral inspector is likely to be continually and closely in touch with the school and may have time to spend a day or even days in the school. But such support tends to be given to meet special and urgent problems facing the school. The support given is certainly in the field of management but it does not usually relate in any systematic way to previous course attendance, even though the head concerned may have been on a management course. Generally speaking, advisers tend to concentrate their support on schools where major issues such as contraction or, still more, possible closure are arising. In the former case, the need for staff redeployment brings both advisers and administrators right into curriculum analysis and planning. In the latter case, both staff structures in the continuing school and staff redeployment from the closing school bring about similar involvement. The officer time involved is great and reduces the opportunities for involvement in support for systematic training and development, whether pre-course or post-course. However, in Chapter Five we give examples of experiments which attempt to link work on urgent issues of this kind directly to training.

As experience with the new regional courses builds up, authorities are no doubt finding ways to enter more fully into course planning with the providers. This in turn will facilitate consultations on pre-course arrangements, the introduction into the course of the participants' actual problems, and post-course support for developments stimulated by the course. However the circumstances we have described begin to reveal an issue which we have increasingly recognised as basic to our study, namely the ability of advisers to provide the kind of help heads need:

> since experienced advisers must occupy a key position in this whole structure of support for management training and development, the problem of creating effective links between training and management performance in the school is not easily solved without careful and systematic planning to make best use of their limited time and to augment this with additional support from other sources.

Support From Providing Institutions

As with the authorities, practice amongst providers is varied and subject to rapid development. Earlier in this Chapter, the NDC survey of training provision made brief reference to the general position. Our own experience is necessarily limited to fewer contacts with providing institutions. Because of the very speedy response required to implement the national training initiative in 1984/85, few if any providing institutions would claim to offer a comprehensive range of support. There is in any case a limit to what providing institutions might usefully do alone. This is not so much a question of resource as one of partnership. Practical and effective support for training can only be given in active association with the LEA.

We set out below examples of various types of support which we encountered in our contacts with providing institutions. We offer these as a sample of what is to be found.

Pre-course activities

All the courses we contacted have some written information available to members before the course. Apart from a letter of welcome and administrative details of course organisation, this usually included some statement of course aims.

Many, but not all, hold special pre-course meetings to allow a further exchange of information. Two courses we visited arranged personal interviews between the course directors and each member. In one case this focussed in the main on an exchange of information about the range of experiences the course would provide and the particular interests and requirements of the course member. These interviews are now being redeveloped to consider particular areas of management practice which might be worked on during the course. In the other case, two interviews, spaced over several weeks and linked to the completion of a short school review questionnaire, allowed a more detailed exploration of broader managerial and educational issues relevant to the head and the school.

Others place varying degrees of emphasis on pre-course reading. In one case, where a special 'course reader' had been prepared, including extracts from journals, national reports and working documents drawn from schools, pre-course reading was substantial and well integrated with activities on the courses.

Preparatory tasks are more common than significant reading assignments. The most common task is the preparation of a case study to be presented within an early module of the course. Others require the collection of information or documents for use on the course such as student profiles, surveys of resource allocation, reports to governors. Occasionally some form of self-analysis is encouraged, through a short written statement or through the completion of a special questionnaire or assessment form.

In general, pre-course support by providers is focussed largely on preparations for taking part in the course: a kind of 'course homework'. There are examples of interviews and other activities where the purpose is to determine the specific personal and institutional requirements for training but in our experience these are less common.

Post-course activities

Where a course has been successful in generating interest and enthusiasm, there is a natural tendency for members to seek to continue the association with the institution and with each other. In consequence, post-course evaluation often shows up a request for some form of reunion which might be arranged on a termly or yearly basis. Some providers use these occasions to promote further professional activities. However, they are seldom used to stimulate the transfer of training experiences into management practice in the school.

One well established training programme, recognising the inherent difficulties of a policy of continuing reunions over a lengthy period as the number of cohorts increase, encourages members to establish their own informal networks of contacts to facilitate mutual support in the implementation of new management skills. In other cases more organised forms of mutual support are provided through small professional seminar groups meeting once or twice each term for informal discussions of issues arising.

In one interesting development, the provider organised a day meeting for the deputies of heads who had recently completed a course to familiarise them with the nature of the training and of likely outcomes.

In only one case did we find a systematic programme of personal debriefing, conducted by the course director, linked to a further, lengthy period of planned management action in the school. Here the provider was working in close relationship with the authority.

Practice in Industry and Commerce

The provision of management training and the promotion of management development within the education profession is of relatively recent origin. There exists within industrial and commercial enterprises a considerably greater accumulated experience within the field. We therefore sought and were offered recommendations as to where best practice might be found within the private sector and subsequently investigated such practice with particular attention to attempts at promoting transfer of learning from training events to effective action on the job.

Six significant contributory elements may be identified as of crucial relevance to the support of effective training: pre-course briefing, preparation, course design, post-course debriefing, follow-up and the organisational context within which training takes place.

Briefing procedures

These are wide-spread, although taking a variety of forms. Most course providers publish information documents well in advance giving details of the purpose and content of courses. In some cases these are used as the basis for discussion between nominating managers and prospective participants. At some such briefing meetings, the needs of the participant in terms of 'self' and of 'the job' are discussed with a mutual exchange of perceptions. Some course providers, however, take the process further, engaging in consultation with participants in order to find ways of meeting needs identified through the regular appraisal procedures of the company. The negotiation of a personal course contract with the participant is the logical extension of this process adopted by at least one company.

Preparation

This clearly begins with the process of briefing outlined above. It is consolidated and taken further, however, by a number of course organisers in ways designed to secure a commitment to, and active engagement in, learning specifically related to personal and organisational need. All the providers of courses reviewed send some form of letter to individual participants, providing further information and inviting or specifying the completion of one or more pre-course tasks. Reading lists are generally seen as ineffective and are seldom supplied. In one example the participants are asked to select an optional study, to prepare a statement of personal learning objectives for the course and to complete a time-use log for four days immediately prior to the course. Another provider sends a battery of preparatory questions to each course member's immediate superior for use with the course member. A more sophisticated method, embodying the same principle, involves the provision of pre-course packages of exercises which the participants can complete only with the active co-operation of their superiors; the results form a basis for activity during the first part of the course. The provision of a floppy disk of inter-active video exercises, in the case of another course, enables completion of the first training module before assembling for off-the-job sessions. This latter tactic was adopted by the provider as a specific response to the large numbers of participants who had previously arrived at the course with no knowledge of why they had 'been sent'; it was designed to make it difficult for participants and those who nominated them to avoid serious thought as to the purpose of course attendance and what might be learned.

Perhaps the most powerful examples of preparation for effective learning leading to action at the workplace are those which carry the kind of processes outlined above to the point where the course member is enabled to create a personal learning plan. At least two independent management colleges have invested considerable resources in this approach, in one case in co-operation with the Manpower Services Commission. The focus in this example is upon the manager's personal learning style, its strengths and weaknesses. Prior to a week's residential course, participants conduct a self-assessment using various diagnostic instruments, reflective writing and discussion with peers and with superiors. In this way they come to the course with some understanding of the practical issues relevant to their own development. The 'course' is then devoted to further diagnosis and to the development of action plans designed to enable participants when back at work to tackle difficulties revealed by the process.

Course design

This remains a topic of immediate concern to course providers and reveals a very wide range of approach and practice with regard to both content and method. A large number of courses continue to be based upon the commonly held view that the manager's job can be described as the exercising of a set of discrete component skills. Development of these skills through a series of planned course activities is then seen as an appropriate way in which to attempt to develop managerial competence. However, an increasing number of trainers are adopting approaches based upon the recognition that a manager's development is a continuous and personal process in which the experience of the manager at work and the ability to learn from it are crucial. In practice the conceptual distinction between the two approaches is frequently less apparent, with course designers mixing elements from both. There is nevertheless a growing belief that specific direct attention to each individual's experience of managing in a particular working context is essential. With that belief comes an increasing emphasis upon managers taking personal responsibility for their own development and an active part in identifying their own needs.

The following are examples we found of strategies aimed at integrating training with the on-going managerial responsibilities of participants:

- job-specific training related to precisely identified task requirements of different managerial roles within an organisation;
- use of managers' current work assignments as the basic material for the training activity;
- insistence by the trainers that all requests for new, job-specific training must be considered within a three-day, full-time

'problem analysis' session between the senior management making the request and the trainers;
- the use of 'job conferences' to bring together managers from different units with similar responsibilities to share problems and to identify possible means of meeting them.

An alternative strategy is to allow and plan for adaptation within a general training activity to meet the individual needs of participants. The simplest example of this can be seen in a modular designed course where individuals select the modules they wish to take up, or where the trainer uses the early part of the course to aid the process of selection, in at least one case making use of repertory grid techniques.

A more radical development is that of providing training events for working teams rather than for individuals drawn from them. Examples of this approach are few, but at least two major management training institutions are now developing courses for such teams, where the real issues and difficulties which the team faces can be tackled.

Debriefing

Debriefing procedures are said to be common but rarely appear to go beyond registering the return of the manager from a course with the most general of questions about its usefulness. At best, it seems, managers may be offered a one-off chance to say what new approaches or procedures they would be interested in adopting in the light of their course experience. Even when careful pre-course briefing has been undertaken, debriefing may consist of no more than a passing exchange in the corridor. We found one example of positive debriefing where regular weekly mutual review meetings were established between course members and their superiors.

The concept of debriefing is significant only in the context of a real commitment to improved action at the place of work. Only then will it lead to effective support for the training experience.

Follow-up procedures

These appear to be as rare in the commercial and industrial sector as in education. Even where they exist, there is little evidence that they are of much value in supporting managers' continued learning or their efforts to put into effect what they have learned.

Where attempts are made to engender follow-up activity on the job, they commonly involve the formulation of an 'action plan'. In such cases the trainer will usually accept responsibility for ensuring that the plan is completed by the course member and may assist in its formulation. However, the evidence indicates that the provision of support, or even a monitoring function, during implementation presents a major unresolved problem. Perhaps the most serious attempt to support the implementation of action plans involves course tutors becoming consultants during the period of implementation. In the example we encountered, the consultants also have a brief to define further training needs of participants and others in the organisation. The scheme is still in its infancy and has yet to be evaluated.

In the small number of cases where action plans appear to have been successfully implemented, one or more of three conditions were met. The most important of these was the involvement of the participant's own manager in active support for the process of implementation by such means as the setting of a time-scale and of monitoring progress. In one organisation in which no immediate superior is available, circulation of the participant's course evaluation report or action plan to regional managers provided an alternative strategy and in another company action plans devised by task teams formed a basis for analysis of further group training needs.

A second relevant factor was the degree to which course providers managed to secure commitment to later action either by pairing participants in 'contracts for action', with each other and the course tutor, or by pairing participants for mutual support purposes beyond the course and ensuring that the plans contained schedules for action and report.

A third factor is the ability of the course organiser to continue to provide a resource bank of further information and activities after the course.

Whilst reunion meetings of course members are generally seen as serving little effective purpose, deliberate attempts are made by some course providers to foster informal networks of contact between participants to provide mutual support. Pairing arrangements of the kind mentioned above may also be related to small group meetings of participants initiated by course providers. The success of such arrangements, however, may depend upon reasonable travelling distances between participants' places of work.

Organisational context

Throughout our discussions with representatives of industry and commerce there emerged two seemingly incompatible principles: on the one hand, the crucial importance of the course participant's own manager in ensuring effective outcomes of training was constantly stressed; on the other hand we identified a growing emphasis upon the importance of individuals accepting personal responsibility for their own development.

The extent to which management training and development activities are in practice carefully integrated with the functional and hierarchical structures of organisations varies very considerably. In some, regular appraisal or performance review procedures, sometimes involving target setting, form the basis of discussion relating to training and development needs. In others, an ad hoc liaison between trainer or course organiser and the course member's immediate superior is created at the time of recruitment to a course. In many, the lack of effective involvement on the part of the manager directly responsible for the participant's on-going work substantially nullifies the efforts of the trainer. The difficulty created by the lack of any on-site superior for newly-trained managers in one organisation has led to a specific review of company strategy to support follow-up activity after course attendance.

In apparent contrast, a number of companies, including some widely respected for the quality of their management and management training, are placing much increased responsibility upon individual managers to say what further training or development activity they require for themselves. They assert that the ultimate responsibility for the effectiveness of training rests with the individual. This view is reflected in the increasing use of self-development materials and activities to assist managers in their efforts to manage more effectively. However, this approach is grounded in the careful analysis of working experience, and this still requires others to provide feedback and perspective. Moreover, action must still take place within the working context, whatever its particular hierarchical structure. Thus in both respects the involvement of the individual's own manager is still essential.

The complex nature of headteacher accountability makes it difficult to apply in an unmodified way procedures and relationships based on the notion of line management. However, similar difficulties apply also to many senior managers in industry and commerce. Even in these cases, where line management relationships are tenuous, management training must operate within a clear organisational context. The responsibility remains with those in key superior positions to provide continuing support and a challenge to action. This is still a crucial element in determining the effectiveness of such training.

References

ARGYRIS, C & SCHON, D 1974 *Theory in practice: increasing professional effectiveness* London: Jossey Bass

KOLB, D & FRY, R 1975, 'Towards an applied theory of experiential learning' in C Cooper (ed) *Theories of group processes* London: Wiley

OAKESHOTT, M 1967 'Learning as teaching' in R S Peters (ed) *The concept of education* London: Routledge & Kegan Paul

CHAPTER TWO

A Planning Framework for Training and Support at the Local Level

The basic recommendation of the report is that LEAs and providers should, at the local level, adopt a two stage strategy in developing management training for heads so that it can make a more effective contribution to the broader programmes of management development which local education authorities might seek to implement. These two stages are: to consolidate arrangements for effective briefing and support for action in school after training; experimentation with different forms of training. In this chapter we consider the elements of local planning which are necessary to consolidate existing provision.

Establishing a Joint Plan

Some heads will come to the training experience with a clear concept of the need to link training to developments in management practice in the school. Others will be less committed to specific initiatives and will be looking only for exposure to new ideas and information. Whatever the state of readiness of each participant, there is a good chance that, sooner or later during the training experience, the practical implications of personal and institutional development will be perceived and accepted. In anticipation of this, it is essential that plans are made to help heads make good practical use of the new ideas, skills and knowledge acquired. Yet in all local education authorities the pressure upon advisory and support services has increased in recent years and the resource available to help heads make good use of training is strictly limited. It is especially important therefore that the available resource is effectively deployed through well laid plans.

Heads will need help (perhaps on a mutual basis) in drawing out the implications of personal development for changes in their management of the school and improvement in the quality of the education it provides. To achieve this linkage between management training and management action, a planning framework is needed to draw together all those elements which require coordination and collaboration between LEAs and providing institutions.

This planning framework we have called the Joint Plan and the elements which require coordination are:

- course design – to ensure a common understanding of its purposes and its organisation;
- recruitment and the process of negotiation with participants – to ensure a continuous concern, before, during and after the course, with the links between the training experience and the intended outcomes;
- support for subsequent management action.

We will review these various elements in turn, indicating the main points requiring consultation and coordination. However, we hold some general assumptions about the nature of this planning framework which must first be made clear.

The Joint Plan in Context

Already, informal machinery exists in all regions to facilitate consultations between LEAs and providers. Wherever possible in this chapter, we draw on examples of good working arrangements for the various elements of the Joint Plan. However, in our experience, it is difficult to achieve a fully integrated plan. When representatives of LEAs and providing institutions attend consultative meetings, their main preoccupation is the provision of the training experience itself and planning levels of recruitment. This is especially true for activities launched as a result of the national initiative following DES circular 3/83: LEAs and providers combine to produce courses which qualify for the expenditure of the available funds. We do not wish to undervalue the current level of cooperation. LEAs see benefit in school management training; they work with providing institutions to provide an acceptable course and they recruit suitable participants. Through this joint action, some measure of quality control is being exercised to ensure that the courses offer relevant experiences.

However, if the training is to be effective as well as relevant, it must be linked positively to educational outcomes in the school. The Joint Plan must adopt a wider focus than the course itself. Providers must be prepared to adjust their programmes to meet specific areas of individual need, once these are identified, and to encourage participants to take personal responsibility for subsequent initiatives. LEAs must give serious consideration to the problem of support for pre-course preparations and post-course activities and commit resources accordingly. The effective allocation of responsibility for these various actions between LEA officers, staff of providing institutions and the participants themselves will depend upon their having a common view of the whole process and in particular the linkage between training and school improvement. In making our recommendations concerning the Joint Plan and its various elements, we are guided by four concepts:

Effective training

All courses provide access to new ideas, skills and knowledge and the chance to share experiences with other heads. But this alone is no guarantee of effectiveness. Effective training relates to subsequent action: action in terms of personal management development and in terms of improvements in the educational service which the school provides for its community. However interesting a course may be, however well presented, it will have no lasting effect upon its members unless they are able to make use of the experience in practical terms. Ideas without action atrophy.

Individual responsibility

Each head, as an experienced professional, is in the end personally responsible for the practical outcomes of training. The greatest resource for effective mid-career professional learning lies within the learner's own creative abilities and individual sense of responsibility, commitment and purpose. So too, in the final analysis, it is the responsibility of each participant to determine the usefulness of the experience and apply it. The purpose of external support in organising preparation and follow-up activities is to assist heads in discharging this responsibility. It is this alone which makes the notion of support a practical proposition.

Learning from experience

To a large extent, experienced professionals are capable of sustaining their own development through systematic reflection upon their experience as they formulate, re-formulate or consolidate their understanding of what they do and how they work. Experiential learning of this kind forms the basis of managerial change and development irrespective of any attempts to introduce formal training into the process. However, where training is introduced, the total programme, including arrangements for preparation and follow-up, should enhance this process of experiential learning and draw upon it to ensure an effective and practical outcome.

School improvement

The quality of education provided by a school is not a stable factor. Its maintenance and development rely on the efforts of its whole community – pupils, parents, teachers and others. But an active, reflective head is the key figure, working with the staff to improve the school. This concept of school improvement as a constant professional effort is the starting and finishing point for the Joint Plan. Training must be seen as an optional 'booster loop' supporting an independent process of school improvement.

The planning framework must therefore place training programmes within this broader context of personal development and management action in response to the requirements of the process of school improvement. The reader should refer to Diagram 1 in reading the sections which follow:

Diagram 1: The Joint Plan in Context

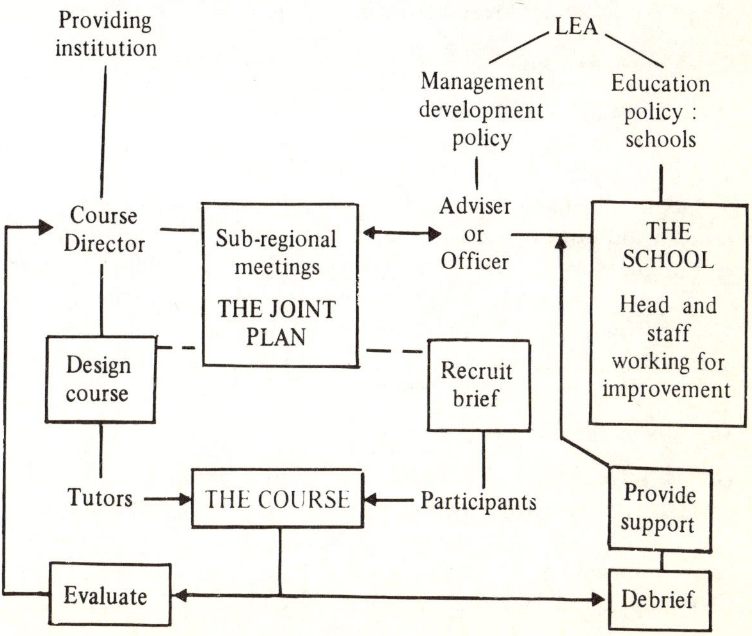

Practical Constraints on Planning

Our immediate purpose is to propose only what is feasible in current conditions. Whilst we believe there are positive steps which can be taken to improve the effectiveness of training, we recognise there are practical constraints. Nothing is gained from ignoring these. Before embarking on the details of the Joint Plan, it is useful to list some of the constraints here:

Course provision

Despite the proliferation of school management courses in recent years there is, in practice, a limited choice for any LEA. This is especially the case where the authority wishes to engage fully in consultations to influence the design of the course. Consequently, there is a tendency to produce a multi-purpose course based on a generalised assessment of training needs and covering a reasonable spread of requirements (usually including a series of modules on specific management topics together with some space for individual projects). Therefore, arrangements for pre-course preparation and post-course support need to be flexible. We do not attempt to design a complete 'package' of supporting activities, but rather a set of options to be deployed according to need.

Recruitment and briefing

Precisely targeted recruitment is difficult, partly because of these constraints on course provision and partly because information on the specific needs of individual heads is not easily available. Consequently, elaborate check-lists or guidelines would offer little to most authorities without major changes in their management development systems. What is needed for immediate use is a simplified approach, in which the essential element is the opportunity for a face-to-face discussion of the appropriateness of training and the purposes to which it will be put.

Subsequent action

Heads have limited time to devote to training. Even when replacement costs are available, there are many responsibilities which cannot be set aside when attending a part-time course. Supporting activities must be well chosen, directly relevant and give clear support to the individual head and school. If industrial management training is a guide, helping managers find time to implement the results of training poses a very difficult problem. It deserves very careful consideration.

Regional planning duties

Officers and advisers too have many demands on their time and cannot be expected to be constantly available for regional planning, course design and organising support for training. Our recommendations for regional planning must be simple and with a clear sense of purpose. Regional meetings should be restricted to the broad policy questions: the nature of the course, the types of support to be provided and levels of recruitment. Given the pressure on officer time, some difficult decisions must be made on its deployment beyond this. For example, authority involvement is crucial to recruitment, briefing and post-course support; it is less important in the detailed process of course design.

The Course Design Phase

We are not concerned here with the procedures for course design, nor do we wish to discuss the details of course content. However, there are certain decisions about the specific purposes of training and the organisation and management of the design team which have implications for the other elements of the Joint Plan. These are matters which must be well coordinated if authorities are to be expected to provide appropriate support before and after training.

Assumptions about the Purposes of Training

We have already indicated that constraints of course provision are likely to lead local consortia to produce multi-purpose courses covering a range of assumptions about the purposes of training. Nevertheless, the main thrust of the course needs to be discussed early in the planning cycle, since different assumptions require different types of support.

One common assumption is that training should focus on the acquisition of management expertise which can be expressed as a set of technical skills. It follows that the skills required can be determined partly from the job specification of headship and partly from an understanding of the functions of management in a broader occupational context. Training modules would therefore be devoted to skills such as strategic planning, resource control, staff appraisal, delegation.

A second assumption focusses on practical problem solving. Here the emphasis is much more on an individual identification of the training task with support provided for the problem solving process and the more generalised skills of solving problems and implementing solutions.

A third assumption is that management training should focus on personal development, helping each participant to increase self awareness and sensitivity to managerial and professional issues. Success might be measured in terms of personal learning styles, responsiveness to the needs of subordinates and the ability to recognise personal strengths and weaknesses.

It goes without saying that each of these assumptions will lead to a different training experience. They also imply different approaches to preparation and follow-up. For example, meeting a technical deficit through training requires a careful and accurate diagnosis of individual need before the course begins and close personal support for the practical application of these skills once acquired. Problem solving, on the other hand, can be dealt with more generally relying on support for small groups, provided a realistic assessment is made of the implementation strategy to be adopted in each case.

The early sub-regional meeting must explore these issues. LEAs will wish to match their intended recruitment policy with the broad intentions of the course. They will also need to make a provisional assessment of the requirements for support and indicate the level of provision they can achieve. It must be recognised that the provision of training opportunities often has its own internal dynamic. In part this stems from the deeply entrenched tradition of syllabus writing. This may give a course the appearance of a technical specification model, although one would need to be sure that the syllabus was derived from a realistic job analysis rather than the readily available and 'teachable' knowledge. In part, it stems from what might be termed a homeostatic factor in regional training programmes (see Diagram 2).

There is nothing necessarily wrong with this model as far as it goes but, in practice, it lacks any emphasis on the development of lasting practical outcomes for the course members. Follow-up is deflected largely towards evaluation (based on immediate reactions) in order to determine further patronage and re-design.

Diagram 2: Homeostasis in the System of Course Provision

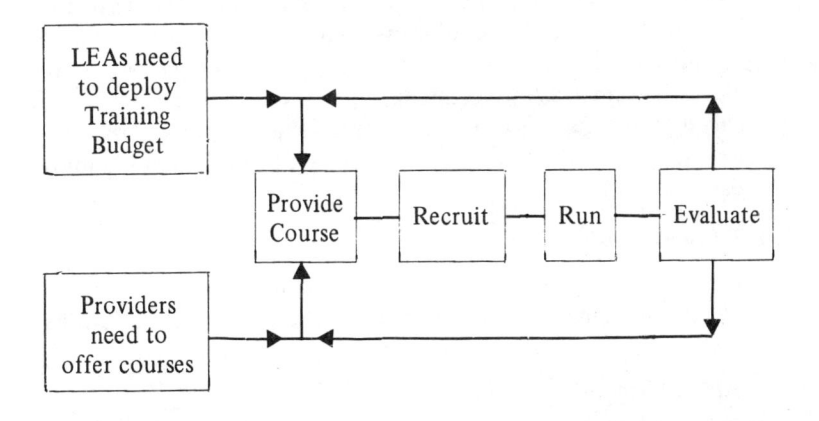

```
┌──────────────┐
│ LEAs need    │
│ to deploy    ├──────┐   ┌────────────────────────────────┐
│ Training     │      ▼   ▼                                │
│ Budget       │   ┌─────────┐  ┌───────┐ ┌─────┐ ┌──────────┐
└──────────────┘   │ Provide │  │Recruit│ │ Run │ │ Evaluate │
                   │ Course  ├──┤       ├─┤     ├─┤          │
┌──────────────┐   └─────────┘  └───────┘ └─────┘ └──────────┘
│ Providers    │      ▲   ▲                                │
│ need to      ├──────┘   └────────────────────────────────┘
│ offer courses│
└──────────────┘
```

The Course Design Team

The second issue which needs to be considered at the initial planning meeting is the composition of the design team and its schedule for developing the programme.

Most providers accept the need for close consultation in the design and organisation of management courses. Many go beyond committee consultation, often recruiting experienced heads to take responsibility for course design. There are strong arguments for avoiding individual responsibility for course design (whoever the individual may be) and establishing a mixed team to reflect not only the experience of headship but of designing courses for mid-career professionals. LEA advisers and officers, heads and members of staff of the providing institutions all have something to offer.

Unless the course format relies heavily on sessions planned around visitors 'speaking to a title' or training modules bought or borrowed 'off the shelf' from outside agencies, course design can be a time consuming affair. But effective school management training requires a custom built design which should make only marginal use of external speakers and packages in offering an integrated training experience. Consequently, the question of design time is quite important. Our own experience, confirmed by other providers, is that the resource required is in the order of magnitude of one man-year to design a new course of the scope and quality required for a twenty day basic course. Thus, two or three heads seconded for one term and supported by a course director might be expected to undertake the design of a new course (as at Bristol). Alternatively, a joint authorities team of advisers, heads and deputies, working part-time with the course director, might need six to nine months to achieve the same (as at Nottingham). Obviously, this time can be reduced with experience or if the course is a redevelopment. But design time should not be under-estimated in the initial planning phase.

The Course Design Schedule

A clear timetable is needed for course design if the other elements of the Joint Plan are to be properly coordinated. The following points are the main factors to be taken into account:

The initial brief

This should be worked out in consultation with the sub-regional committee or consultative group. These discussions should result in an agreed written brief for the design team.

Allocation of responsibilities

The division of labour within the team will depend upon its size and the structure of the course. At Nottingham, for example, three separate sub-groups each produce a training module. However, the Nottingham team recognises the importance of whole team review for all modules in order to ensure an integrated course. All components will need extensive revision in these early stages.

An interim report

A report should be made to the sub-regional committee once details of the course outline are clear but before course administration begins.

The administration phase

Once the course structure is agreed, course administration requires a greater involvement by staff of the providing institution, organising the printing of course materials and programmes, booking accommodation etc.

A final briefing session

A meeting for all course tutors (usually drawn from the design team) is necessary before the course begins.

Course Evaluation

Arrangements for course evaluation should be built in from the beginning of the design phase. The NDC has now produced detailed advice on course evaluation and we do not intend to repeat it here. However, there are three separate functions of evaluation during the life of the course and the distinction must be made clear within the Joint Plan:

- the first function of evaluation is to enable the programme to be adjusted as it runs, in order to ensure that its objects are achieved. Providing there has been adequate negotiation with the participants concerning the practical reasons for undertaking training, interim evaluations can help to keep things on track;
- the second function is a natural continuation of the first and enables individual participants to evaluate the experience and to assess its potential for implementation personally or by the school as a whole;
- the third function is the more familiar one of assessing the worth of the training experience for future use with other people.

Recruitment and the Process of Negotiation

Recruitment is the beginning of a comprehensive sequence of actions in and around the training experience which can be conveniently dealt with in three phases: in school before training, during training, in school after training.

These phases are more than just divisions of time. They indicate shifts in perspective. When it is decided that the normal process of professional development should be boosted by attendance at an external course in school management, there is a clear intention to effect a temporary shift in perspective. The head takes a deliberate decision to withdraw from the normal preoccupations of headship in order to focus on particular aspects of school management. This deliberate withdrawal into a separate, temporary system can help heads rethink their approach to school management. But the world of training, however interesting and valuable an experience in its own right, can often remain a very separate experience from the world of work. Steps must be taken before, during and after the course to facilitate the move from the school to the training experience and back again, and to ensure that the different perspectives do not remain separate and unconnected. It is generally accepted that the training experience is relevant to the extent that it gets the participant thinking about work in school. But the other half of the connection requires the head to think about the training experience whilst in school before and after the course. The recommendations below are designed to facilitate this process.

In School Before Training

For the head, this phase begins with recruitment. This may be as a result of the local education authority extending a direct invitation to attend the course or it may be at the head's own initiative. In either case, the decision to attend should involve a full and open discussion of the purposes of training in terms of personal development and school improvement. We do not offer any elaborate procedures here. They will vary according to circumstances in each authority: the existence of any system of career review and appraisal, for example. Recruitment policy will in any case be a function of several factors: training budget, assessment of heads' needs and the availability of suitable courses. This will necessarily be a process of approximation as the various claims are sifted through a series of informal contacts and discussions. However, once the list of potential candidates begins to firm up, the discussions between LEA officers and heads should cover three main elements:

Matching

A head's training requirements are identified and appropriate training opportunities located. The discussion must start with an open exchange on the purposes of training and the appropriateness of the available courses. No good is achieved by sending heads on courses when they do not know why they have been selected.

Briefing

Once a broad agreement has been reached on the potential value of a particular piece of training, the discussion should be extended to explore the implications in greater detail. More will be said later of discussions with course tutors, but here we assume that the LEA officer is sufficiently well informed of the details of the training programme to engage in this preliminary briefing.

Briefing implies more than information. Both parties should discuss each other's expectations and requirements and be prepared to respond in a practical manner. This exchange lays the foundations for the third part of the discussion.

Forecasting

Once the purposes of training have been established consideration must be given to the likely outcomes for management in the school. The possible resource implications should be examined now before the course. It will probably be necessary at this point to draw in other members of staff who may be subsequently involved in management changes in the school.

Arrangements for cover

The routine provision of a supply teacher for the days a head is absent is not in itself sufficient. A supply teacher cannot replace a head. Thought must be given to the reallocation of management duties amongst senior staff. This may require a different type of replacement or a higher level of funding, both of which the national initiative allows when releasing headteachers. The reallocation of part of the head's duties during the period of training and any associated periods of school-based study is important, not only to ensure full participation in training, but as a first step in allocating responsibilities for action after training.

During the Course

Preparatory exercises

The bulk of pre-course exercises, where they exist, are used to prepare for learning activities within the modules. However, in addition to this they can be used to encourage and facilitate the briefing procedures described above. Examples are given in Chapter One of activities used in this way by industrial trainers. These might be especially useful in promoting joint action inside the school with senior members of the staff. Similarly pre-course information documents or familiarisation meetings can include a section to promote briefing and forecasting discussions. However, the scope for this type of preparatory action will vary from course to course.

Personal contracts

Obviously, courses have to be planned well in advance of recruitment. Yet participants must be given an opportunity to influence events. This is especially true for those elements of training which emphasise individual projects. However, participants will also need to think carefully about other aspects of the training and their practical implications for school management, and integrate this within a personal programme of reflection and action. Course directors should pick up the briefing discussions concerning the expectations which each of the participants has before the course. We use the phrase 'personal contract' to define these negotiations through which a sense of joint task and common purpose is established between provider and participants. These negotiations may begin with individual meetings; some directors visit each participant in school to discuss the course. Nevertheless group discussions should also be arranged so that intentions can be shared.

Assessing progress

Once the idea of personal contract is well established, it forms the basis for a periodic review of progress and an assessment of the success of the training experience in meeting needs. Linking course evaluation to personal contracts allows a distinction to be made between 'satisfaction' and 'achievement'. Frequently, mid-course or terminal reviews reflect the former rather than the latter. But there are times when the achievement of results can be uncomfortable, when people need to live with uncertainty for a while. In these circumstances, a degree of tension and dissatisfaction may have to be lived through. People can accept this once the purpose of the exercise is clear; they can only assess progress against some previously stated sense of purpose. Of course, if it is not being achieved then the course plans must be changed.

Considering action

The emphasis on personal contracts and stated intentions in reviewing progress is designed to maintain a climate of purpose and action. However, not everyone will be ready from the outset to be committed wholeheartedly to a change in management. Quite properly, they will wish to assess opportunities for change before abandoning the status quo. Nothing is gained in these circumstances by pressing for commitment; instead, participants should be encouraged to make a careful personal assessment of the potential of each new idea or input to the course. After each module or topic, provision should be made for this review. Towards the end of training, the written record of these assessments can be a valuable aid in planning post-course action.

In School After the Course

Action after the course may involve quite ambitious changes in school management. These may require a lengthy period of preparation, trial and implementation, either on a personal basis or involving colleagues in the school. External support for this action is the subject of the next section and the chapters which follow. However, debriefing discussions with LEA officers and colleagues in the school should follow immediately upon the course. The briefing and forecasting discussions may have continued intermittently throughout the period of training as ideas develop. They should now be brought to a conclusion with a review of the action to be taken. This has two aspects.

Implementation

The head should draw up a plan for action. This may be a personal plan for changes in management style, or it may be a corporate plan for new management systems in the school. The authority will already be in touch with these developments through earlier discussions and should be ready to give support where needed. Colleagues in school should be drawn as appropriate into the consideration of the plan.

Dissemination

As a result of the debriefing session and the development of a plan of action, there may well be aspects of the training experience which should be passed on to individual colleagues or the staff as a whole. No doubt this will include a general report to the staff, but there may also be the occasion for an in-house training programme.

Support for Management Action: An Overview

The final element of the Joint Plan is the provision of support for action. This will require detailed planning and organisation, much of which must await the outcome of training and the head's response to it. However, it will be necessary to consider this in broad outline in the initial discussions between the authority and the providing institution. Consequently, we include here an overview of the various types of support which might be included in the Joint Plan, reserving to Chapters Three and Four the further details of each activity.

The kinds of practical response to their training experience which heads will wish to make will vary considerably. Some will wish to engage in a period of systematic reflection before deciding on specific changes, others will be seized with the need for immediate action. The types of action too will vary. We find it useful to make a distinction between personal action, relating to the head's own management performance, and corporate action, where the head will need to involve other members of the school. Both are important and there are many connections between the two. But the distinction provides a useful framework for the consideration of the kinds of support which can be provided.

Support for Personal Action

Here we are concerned with support in the application of newly acquired personal skills, management style, time management, interview techniques. However, the development of personal skills cannot be treated simply as a once and for all exercise. Formal training may focus on specific items, but this should be regarded as a boost to a long term process and not as a single cycle event. Support therefore must include help in developing the habit of systematic self-development, focussing directly on the individual experience of headship.

There are several possibilities for support, largely within the head's own sphere of initiative. There is also scope for help and encouragement from the LEA, beginning at the post-course debriefing session. In our own experimental work and in our discussions with others addressing similar issues, we have identified three types of action which offer help. It will be clear from the brief description which follows that they are not mutually exclusive and could easily be put together to form a package. They offer a mixture of individual and group activities. In all cases the major resource is the head's own time and initiative.

Self-development workshops

These short workshop sessions give heads the opportunity to re-assess their development needs, preview a wide range of materials and self-help activities designed to help them take practical action, work out a personal plan and implement it. They are useful in helping heads focus on specific issues from the many which will have been raised in training.

Mutual support groups

The peer group is a major source of support in management development. Heads can meet together in various forms of mutual support group which focus on aspects of mid-career development. We would draw attention to four types of group.

- Professional seminars create opportunities for the detailed analysis of topics of professional concern whilst also providing support of a more personal kind concerning school management performance. Such groups often develop naturally from associations formed during formal training and pick up issues which have been raised there.
- The Cleveland LEA study groups have operated for several years with support from local industrial management trainers. About fifteen heads meet two or three times each term to consider school management issues.
- Professional partnerships, usually between two people, encourage heads to provide mutual support in the assessment of personal performance. Partnerships are frequently advocated for the review of management style and personal relations.
- Peer review audit groups enable heads to work together in small groups to determine criteria for effective management practice and to assess their own performance against them.

Keeping a professional journal

A journal is a valuable aid to systematic reflection upon the stream of events that make up the average day of a head. With practice the journal becomes an important element in planning action as well as reflecting on it.

Support for Corporate or Collective Action

Here we are concerned with heads tackling more complex corporate or collective management issues, for example a major curriculum reorganisation, an appraisal scheme, new patterns of internal or external communication. Innovations of this kind will encounter many obstacles and will need a different kind of support. Essentially the main action will be internal to the school, involving formal and informal discussions, planning groups and development teams, before successful implementation is achieved. However there is a need to provide some external support for the head.

There are four types of external support which are of particular relevance to the head attempting complex corporate change in school management:

The action learning set

This brings together about six managers (not necessarily all heads) each of whom is committed to the solution of a complex problem. The set members provide mutual support throughout the process.

Consultancy

Consultancy appears to be little used in education and is usually expensive. However it can be used as a source of support for heads engaging in planned change. In Chapter Four we list the various consultancy functions and review the sources of support available.

The LEA task group

Special working groups are useful in circumstances where the requirements for corporate action are wider than the school. Increasingly, there is a need for collaboration and coordination between schools (for example, in preparing for a local reorganisation, or developing a consortium solution to problems of curriculum provision). Training programmes do not usually relate directly to such circumstances, but can have a positive influence providing they are planned and organised to do so. Providing that the Joint Plan takes account of the possibility, the opportunity exists for an officer or adviser to convene the heads in order to work together on common problems and plan appropriate action in the schools.

Cascade training

The head's involvement in the provision of training opportunities for others can in some cases be seen as a diversion from school management. However training is of direct relevance to improved management within the head's own school where:
- the head's own attempt to apply new management techniques is dependent upon others on the staff acquiring them too (often the case with management styles);
- the head, perhaps as a result of the training experience, wishes to extend personal responsibility for staff development in the school;
- a major corporate change in school management requires some form of senior management team training.

A training programme of this kind does not need special support activities, but it will need help in the form of in-service funds and perhaps inputs from advisers in designing the programme. However, although there is no need for special support activities, we have felt it necessary to consider the organisational form which this school-focussed training might take and certain factors in the management and development of the programme which will enhance its effectiveness.

CHAPTER THREE
Support for Personal Action

In Chapter Two we gave an overview to the supporting activities which might be considered for inclusion in the Joint Plan. In this chapter we provide more detail on those activities designed to support action taken by heads to improve their own management practice. We aim to give enough detail on each of the options to allow their usefulness to be assessed and to give some idea of what is involved in organising them. In the Annotated Bibliography we list further sources of information for those intending to take up the ideas in practice.

The Management Self-development Workshop

Management courses encourage members to identify personal or institutional development needs. Nevertheless the Joint Plan must take account of the fact that the process may be incomplete at the end of the course, and is, in any case, likely to be forgotten under the pressure of work.

The self-development workshop is designed to help heads continue with this process. It provides additional stimulus and support for individual intiative during the period when the awareness gained from the course might be converted into personal action in school. Note however, that if the workshop is successful, the Joint Plan will also have to provide support for that action when it occurs.

There is already a variety of published materials, mostly in loose-leaf sets, which are designed for this purpose of management self-development. The materials consist of a wide range of questionnaires, diagnostic instruments and analytical and planning procedures. Some twenty-five heads, LEA officers and advisers have helped the project team assess the usefulness of these materials. A record of some of their comments is set out in Chapter Six. Although the materials were not designed with school management specifically in mind, they are of considerable value.

Our experience is that it is best to approach the whole question of continuing self-development through a short experimental workshop. During an initial two-day session, held about three months after the end of training, a group of six heads are introduced, through work in pairs and as individuals, to a pre-selected sample of the materials. They make a selection from these for immediate trial and joint review and are encouraged to amend, rewrite and redesign materials where necessary to render them appropriate to school management. The process is repeated or continued to enable each participant to make a selection of a small number of items for use within a period of some six weeks at school and to produce a written statement of intent about their use. At the end of this period the group reconvenes for a further one or two-day session to review together difficulties, successes and failures experienced and to plan further action as required. An outstanding feature is the wide variety of personal and institutional purposes that may be served within the one workshop.

The Materials

Two collections of materials have provided the majority of items used in pilot workshops of this kind:

- *Management self-development: a practical manual for managers and trainers* (Designed by an Inter-Industrial Training Board Study Group and published by the Manpower Services Commission, 1983);
- *Fifty activities for self-development* A companion volume to *The unblocked manager* by D. Francis and M. Woodcock (Published by Gower, 1982).

The two collections of materials are differently organised, the first under topic headings, the second in relation to potential blockages to managerial competence. Both, however, contain an introduction and guide notes for trainers or users followed by exercises designed by the authors from a wide variety of acknowledged sources. Further details of these and other materials are given in the Annotated Bibliography, but the main topics covered by the materials include:

- Self-assessment: personal focus, work focus, relationship focus;
- Job/Career/Life Planning;
- Managerial Activities, e.g. problem solving, decision making, time management;

- Leadership/Management Style;
- Organisational Climate;
- Power/Authority/Motivation;
- Learning: general self-development, training skills.

None of the items in either collection has been designed for use by headteachers. Some are nevertheless relevant and appropriate as written, whilst a considerable number reveal their commercial or industrial origins in language and terminology. Few, however, embody assumptions entirely inappropriate in an educational context. Some items are intended for use by an individual alone; in some cases it is suggested that subsequent comparison and discussion with a partner will be helpful. Other items are specifically designed as instruments for acquiring feedback from colleagues whilst others depend upon group use for their effectiveness. The range of concerns and activities represented is sufficiently wide to serve the needs of those who have precisely defined purposes as well as those who wish to engage in initial review or diagnosis. There is also a variety of focus from the essentially personal to the wholly institutional.

Reproduction of individual items for training purposes is permitted with appropriate acknowledgement.

Organising the Workshop

General climate

The workshop invites members to evaluate and perhaps redevelop the materials for their own use. This is an important feature, giving an 'experimental' feel which should characterise the approach. It is likely to be experienced as less immediately threatening than, for example, membership of a group sharing personal journals or the initial stages of action learning.

The organisers

It is essential that organisers avoid the role of tutor, management consultant or "expert in education". In the beginning, the appropriate role is closer to information assistant than tutor, since a thorough familiarity with the materials presented and experience of using them is important. The overall approach is an invitation to explore the potential of the materials in the manner of co-researchers.

Experience in pilot workshops indicates that two organisers

working together and sharing the different duties at particular times is likely to be more effective than one person attempting to fulfil all tasks. As the workshop progresses, the organisers will be involved in:
- facilitating the processes of trial, joint review, re-writing and selection within the workshop;
- providing advice with regard to the availability of further materials;
- keeping a record of issues in discussion;
- servicing the practical needs of participants.

Planning the workshop

Apart from the routine tasks – producing a programme, task sheets and joining instructions – there is a major planning job in selecting an initial sample of materials. The size and composition of the sample is quite critical. We have found that twenty to thirty items covering individual and team management development activities is about right.

Recruitment

We assume that recruitment will arise out of course debriefing and may be at the suggestion of either the head or the authority. The experimental nature of the workshop and the emphasis on individual initiative requires voluntary membership by heads who fully understand the purpose in advance. This is reinforced by the joining instructions which give full details of the procedures and the requirements of members.

It is also useful at this stage to give participants the opportunity to complete a 'learning styles questionnaire' since an awareness of personal learning style is useful in selecting development activities.

The first meeting

Presenting the tasks: when the group assembles, each member is given a full list of the materials available and copies of the same twenty-four selected items. The workshop begins with a presentation of the materials and the way in which they are categorised, and may also include explanation of the learning styles questionnaire, the theory upon which it is based and the significance of the results obtained by members.

Reviewing the materials: members working in pairs examine eight items allocated by the organisers in such a way that all twenty-four are covered between the three pairs. Each member is provided with a pro-forma on which to record comments about the potential value of each item and to indicate whether or not it is appropriate for trial, requires further consideration or rewriting, or seems irrelevant or unusable.

Selection and trial: following a meeting of the whole group to share information and initial responses, members select particular items for trial. From this point individual activities begin to vary according to the nature of the choices made. Some members may complete a single lengthy item whilst others may attempt several shorter ones.

Rewriting: a further whole group review session enables members to tell others what they have attempted and to negotiate, for example, collaboration in re-writing or re-designing items. Some members will wish to examine further items which others have described and the organisers may be asked to identify other materials relating to a particular concern or topic. The aim is to enable members to acquire rapidly an awareness of the range of materials and to stimulate consideration of personal and institutional needs.

Planning trial activities: further individually negotiated tasks are followed by the whole group sharing information and ideas. In our experience, this emphasis on individual activity followed by group meetings generates considerable discussion about substantive issues of leadership, management style, decision making, stress, working relationships, etc. The choice of materials for use back at school arises out of this. In the last session, during the afternoon of the second day, members finalise their choices and write a plan of intended action, and share it with the rest of the group and the organisers.

The trial period

Members are asked to use the selected materials on the job for about six weeks. Organisers contact members at least once by telephone to remind them of the forthcoming review session and to assure members that reporting the difficulties encountered will be as valuable as reports of success.

The final review day

Reporting back: we have found it best to begin the final review day with an explicit and formalised mode of reporting. Half an hour is devoted to each report. First, the reporter has ten minutes to give a descriptive account to the whole group of what was attempted, without interruption or comment from the rest of the group. Another member of the group acts as principal listener and at the end of the description has up to five minutes in which to ask questions aimed at clarification of what happened. A further ten minutes is then available for the whole group to ask questions aimed at identifying the most important issues that arise from what the reporter has said. The reporter then has up to a further five minutes in which to restate perceptions, if necessary, and to make observations upon the experience.

Identifying issues: after all members have reported, a subsequent session is devoted to identification of the issues which have emerged. Where members express a desire to take the process further, the organisers may introduce the notion of learning plans and provide examples of them. It is at this point that that the process may become qualitatively different. Materials cease to be central and may come to be seen as useful aids within longer term strategies for learning through action at work.

Further support

Members may decide that the group should continue to meet at intervals as a self-help group. In one case, a member developed a detailed plan for the creation of a group amongst colleagues at work. Another plan involved a pairing partnership with a colleague to provide mutual support and challenge.

Issues Encountered in Workshops

Each member of each workshop will form separate opinions about self-development and will shape a personal response. However, during the pilot workshops the following issues emerged as significant to several members:
- participation in the workshop was itself a powerful incentive or discipline enabling participants to make time *at work* to stand back and examine longer term personal and organisational needs and ways of meeting them;
- in many instances participants involved senior colleagues in school in the development exercise and modified practice in the light of resulting discussion;
- the materials used were frequently described as of less importance in their own right than the shared process of mutual

review which they stimulated; the materials represented a valuable 'neutral territory' in which to begin open consideration of difficult issues;
- rewriting and/or redesigning of materials was undertaken in relation to only a small number of items and only in cases where they were to be offered to participants' colleagues at school; alterations were largely matters of presentation and vocabulary rather than of substance;
- substantive concerns frequently expressed and forming the basis of the selection of items included: management of stress, management of time, conduct and quality of meetings, personal strengths and weaknesses of self and colleagues, team building, personal and organisational blockages to effective management;
- increasingly open sharing of personal difficulties with colleague heads during the workshops was experienced as a valuable form of support;
- the need to formulate a longer term plan or strategy for personal development was perceived as essential by some participants; this would be aided, however, by a continuing supportive structure of the workshop kind.

Mutual Support Groups

The peer group is a major source of support in management development. To this end, heads can meet together in various forms of mutual support group which focus on aspects of mid-career development. Personal mentors in the form of senior heads available to give advice and information have been recommended to us, but we see their value more in relation to the initial stages of headship. Several authorities are now encouraging heads to meet together after training using a variety of organisational structures. We would draw attention to four distinct types of group: the Sussex professional seminar, the Cleveland study group, professional partnership, peer review audit group.

Each focusses on aspects of management performance, but the emphasis varies. It will be a matter of judgement for LEAs, in drawing up the Joint Plan with providers, to determine which type of group will be of value in the particular circumstances.

The Sussex Professional Seminar

This type of group is designed for heads who at the end of a training experience feel the need for a further period of exploration of some of the issues raised before moving to direct action. The professional seminar is organised deliberately in a low key, almost traditional way. It aims to create a relaxed setting which helps heads to consider the need for personal action on their own terms and at their own pace. The strategy is to maintain interest in development rather than to press for an immediate flurry of activity.

Small groups of between five and eight are convened, usually on the initiative of one or two heads. With administrative support and encouragement from the staff of the School of Education, they approach other heads who they feel would form a compatible group. It takes some time to convene the group in this way, but it is important that all the members share a mutual esteem and feel that they have had some part in its initiation. There is no need to secure a long term commitment to membership. Indeed, groups often benefit from a feeling that the decision to meet again is genuinely based on each individual's assessment of the value of the exercise.

Meetings are divided into two parts. The opening session of about an hour is devoted to a professional seminar where one of the members presents a short paper or prepared oral statement on a predetermined topic for discussion and analysis. This is then followed by dinner in a private room and informal conversation ranging across current issues of concern to individual members. This division into two parts is designed to achieve a change in atmosphere, from formal to informal exchange and from general topics to personalised issues. As members gain in confidence in each other, the group provides a valuable source of personal support and professional therapy.

Our experience is that a group, once successfully established, might expect a lifespan of one to two years, meeting twice termly. Sometimes external circumstances will force a change in membership on the group; this is difficult to accommodate with the degree of intimacy which has been developed.

Even where the group has been successful, after about two years it may feel that "something else should be put on the agenda". Suggestions may be made to invite outside speakers or that guests should be permitted. Since the group is autonomous, it will do whatever it decides. However in our opinion such a development is a mistake for all but the occasional meeting and the very special guest. The whole climate of mutual confidence is broken by the introduction of the stranger and the professional discipline of the analysis of the prepared paper is weakened. One group embarked upon the development of management training for heads of department. This proved a most valuable experience for the heads, but the level of commitment to this new activity inevitably varied, and it soon became a separate exercise.

The professional seminar, with its limited aims and minimal time commitment, must be assessed as worthwhile in itself to justify its continuation. The desire to incorporate other activities is an indication that the life of the seminar is coming to an end. But this should be interpreted positively; a request for 'more action' may indicate that other forms of support may now be appropriate.

The Cleveland Study Groups

The Cleveland Study Groups are in many ways similar to the Sussex Professional Seminars. However, there are several distinctive features. The following description is drawn from an account given to us by a member of the Wilton Group.

The group has been in existence for seven years with a membership of ten primary and secondary heads, one LEA Adviser and two industrial training officers from the nearby ICI works. Throughout this period, the Group has regularly held half day meetings on a monthly basis. Each meeting is devoted to a single management topic of mutual interest and concern. Examples include leadership skills, management of time, managing effective relationships and problem ownership. In the early years, the meetings were usually held in the afternoon, preceded by lunch.

After about five years of regular meetings the group reviewed progress. Members recognised the value of the group in raising their interest and awareness of management issues. They also appreciated the opportunity for informal discussion with colleagues whom they came to know well and respect over this lengthy period. However, they also recognised that they were not capitalising fully on the potential of the group meetings to influence their management practice. All too often they would return to school after considering an important topic of clear relevance to their work as heads only to become immersed once again in the routines and daily pressures of school life. The common problem of converting new experiences into effective management practice was present here as in most other management training.

The recognition of this problem led the group to make changes in the organisation. Members continued to meet on a monthly basis but meetings were switched to a 9 a m start so that the informal discussions over lunch did not take precedence over the planned business of the day and members could come fresh to the group rather than arrive after a busy morning. The length of meeting is now varied according to the needs of the topic and may on occasion last all day.

The group now conducts annual reviews of the studies which have been undertaken. From these reviews it makes specific plans for 'cascade training' where this seems appropriate to the topic under consideration. This training is usually directed towards the deputy heads in each school in order to increase the likelihood of action inside the school to improve management practice. Group members also make specific commitments to follow-up action between meetings on aspects of the monthly topic.

In these ways the group has managed to increase its sense of purpose and action and to sustain the interest and commitment of its members for a further two years. Unlike the Sussex group the Wilton group is geared to a continuous existence.

In Cleveland new groups are now beginning to form, not always on precisely this model. For example, multi-disciplinary groups drawing members from industry and commerce as well as from schools are convened for special study sessions on topics of common concern. These groups frequently lead to the establishment of working parties producing detailed reports and recommendations for policy and practice.

Professional Partnership

Perhaps the most popular form of support amongst the authorities we contacted is some arrangement for heads to work together in twos or threes. We give details of one organised scheme identified by the National Development Centre.

The professional partnership programme, developed by Hamilton Associates for elementary schools in the United States, is a process designed to help heads define their organisational and managerial skills. An introductory workshop explains the process to interested heads and helps them choose partners. Heads then work in pairs to provide mutual support and assistance in the process of self-assessment aimed at identifying personal managerial styles. Partners then continue to help each other deal with specific practical management problems. The director of the programme convenes the plenary workshops and acts as a process consultant to every pair of partners, helping them feed back information to each other. The length of the programme can be varied; in practice, programmes have ranged from four to seven months, including about seven days attendance at plenary workshops.

The introductory workshop

This usually lasts for two days and deals with the following topics: orientation; selection of partners; training in the administration and interpretation of management and leadership style questionnaires; development of an agreement between partners with regard to the nature of the observations and enquiries each will make of the other's management practice; training in observational techniques; training in giving feedback.

School visits

These are arranged between partners. Data relating to specific aspects of the host's management activities are gathered by the combination of questionnaires, interviews and direct observation agreed at the workshop. The visitor prepares a summary of findings which is first discussd with the director who advises on the best method of reporting to the partner. When both partners have completed this reciprocal process, the 'mutual feedback session' takes place in the presence of the director acting as consultant. Each partner then considers possible goals for future action in the school.

Goal setting

A two-day workshop is devoted to: review of feedback training; training in goal setting; setting goals and objectives; developing strategies for action; scheduling strategies; negotiating monitoring sessions.

Plans are implemented by participants

They gather additional data if needed and monitor their partner's progress either by telephone or meeting.

Progress reports

Each participant reports progress to the whole group under the supervision of the director at two one-day sessions.

Final evaluation

In a final session, participants report on the completion of their plans and evaluate their level of success.

Recruitment and organisation

Although the initial workshop provides an overview of the scheme, it is important that heads interested in taking part should have an earlier opportunity to be briefed, before any commitment is entered into. Only after heads have had an opportunity to preview some of the diagnostic instruments and assess the demands on their time and effort made by the obligation of partnership, should active recruitment begin. Attendance at the introductory workshop is not a substitute for this briefing process.

If a scheme of professional partnership is envisaged, the sponsors must be satisfied that the level of response will be sufficient to ensure a good choice for pairings and to justify the expenditure of the director's time. On the other hand, a scheme for more than ten pairs is probably beyond the capacities of one consultant in terms of the level of personal attention necessary.

The need for school visits must also be taken into account when considering the geographical area from which participants will be drawn. Whilst pairing is arranged on the basis of self-selection at the introductory workshop, some constraint on choice may be necessary and this will need to be clarified. The success of the scheme depends on a full commitment to the whole cycle of workshops, visits and meetings. Consequently things must be arranged so that this can be achieved with a minimum of disruption to the normal routine.

Peer Review Audit Group

John Heron of Surrey University has developed this form of peer group review, working over the last ten years with doctors, dentists, managers and management trainers. The purpose is to enable practitioners who have no easy access to review by superior to develop techniques of peer-group review on selected aspects of their jobs.

The group can vary in size from a maximum of eight down to a minimum of two. Heron also claims that the method is applicable to hierarchical audit groups of a manager and subordinate with each offering self-assessment and feedback for the other. It would be possible, therefore, for the head to make use of this with deputies.

Heron (1981) defines seven stages in the peer review audit

procedure.

At the first meeting:
- the group identifies the procedures which are central to professional practice and chooses a few of these for the first audit cycle;
- the group clarifies the criteria for good practice and adopts them;
- the group helps each member devise some method of sampling everyday practice in order to assess personal performance.

Between meetings:
- members return to work and for an agreed period undertake the sampling and assessment.

At the second meeting:
- members return to the group and each is invited to report in turn on self-assessment whilst the rest of the group offer critical but, in the end, supportive comment;
- the group undertakes an interim evaluation of the audit procedure and it is modified;
- the second audit cycle is planned.

Heron sees an initial need for a facilitator to introduce the group to this process but assumes that the group will quickly take control, allowing the facilitator to withdraw.

Keeping a Personal Journal

In essence, all that is required here is that the head agrees to maintain a daily, or perhaps weekly record of personal experiences and reflections relating to the work of headship. The act of systematic reflection upon the stream of incidents which make up the average day is a very valuable aid to personal development. However, despite the simplicity of the concept, the act of keeping a journal is not without its difficulties. The very nature of headship makes it difficult to set aside a quiet period on a regular basis for systematic reflection. Moreover, in their early attempts at this kind of reflective writing, heads are often uncertain about what to set down. Support for the process is best provided on a mutual basis with other heads who are embarking on the exercise, so that the experience of writing the journal can be shared.

Accounts of the experiences of two people who kept journals systematically for a significant period are reproduced in Chapter Six. From these and other accounts the following points can be made.

The Process

There are several approaches to keeping a journal which can be adopted. They are not mutually exclusive, but form something of a hierarchy of functions. It is for each individual to choose the approach which fits most easily with personal styles of reflection and with the level of commitment allocated to the activity. The first approach focusses on a reflection on the day's events. The others represent attempts at the analysis of specific aspects of working life. These can be undertaken as isolated exercises but they are best seen as extensions to this basic process of writing about daily events.

Journal as therapy

Keeping a journal can be seen as an antidote to the stresses of a fragmented day. It is one way of putting the day together, coming to terms with the problems faced and the choices made. All that is required here is to sit down and write out the events as they come to mind. For those who find this of value, the process tends to develop quite naturally from this beginning and improve with regular practice. However, an important second step lies in the subsequent analysis of the written record. This can be undertaken in a commonsense way either alone or with the help of a friend or colleague. However the other approaches described below give instances of specific kinds of analysis.

The critical incident diary

The main purpose of this approach is to focus directly on one or two key incidents each day; to record each incident briefly and then to move immediately into an analysis of one's personal response to the event. One method of analysis which has been offered to managers in industry includes the following steps:
- Describe a difficult or significant situation which you had to deal with today;
- How often do you encounter this situation?
- How did you react to it?
- How could you improve the way in which you dealt with it?

It is suggested that this process should take about ten minutes at the end of each day; that it is helpful on occasions to discuss the situation with a colleague; that a periodic review of entries will help focus on the degree to which anything has been learned from the analysis.

Activity analysis

This is a matter of recording what is done at specific regular intervals each day (e.g. every hour or half hour). This helps build up a picture over a number of days of the main activities and how time is spent in pursuing them, particularly in relation to decision making. Usually this type of analysis requires a detailed diary of activities (and interruptions), followed by a weekly assessment of the effective use of time and steps to be taken to improve the situation.

This is a short term exercise which, although useful to repeat from time to time, does not in itself constitute a regular journal. Nevertheless it exemplifies the kind of task-related activity which can be incorporated within the routine of keeping a journal. Indeed, the range of self development exercises and materials which are now available (see the section on "Self Development Workshops") can be most effective if used in conjunction with the keeping of a journal. The regular routine of reflection and analysis involved in maintaining the journal entries provides a controlling context for the choice of self development activities. Thus, on some days the time set aside for the journal would be used in planning further study rather than on reflection.

Timing and Organisation

Any one journal entry will need between fifteen minutes and an hour, depending upon its nature. The journal can be kept on a weekly basis, perhaps using part of the weekend for write up and review. However this would only be feasible if rough notes were kept on a systematic basis at critical times during the week.

Daily entries are often recommended. There is no doubt that daily reflection gives a qualitatively different result providing the time is available; it has the advantage of keeping the reflection close to the action and, if the habit can be maintained, makes systematic reflection a regular part of working life. However there is a danger, if the daily entries become contracted by pressure of other work, or even cancelled for other appointments, that they become perfunctory and superficial, yielding few insights and little analytical material. Perhaps the best combination is one of short daily entries with a longer period of reflection and analysis each week, and regular half term reviews.

The Journal in Context

It might appear that too much emphasis is being placed upon the value of keeping a journal. One or two hours each week is a substantial demand upon the time of a headteacher. However the journal, with its emphasis on reflection, analysis and subsequent action, is a direct manifestation of the learning process of the mid-career professional. For those who find that they are able to keep a journal of this kind over any lengthy period of time, it can prove to be the most valuable aid to professional development; it can provide a routine which becomes the core of personal planning and action. References to journal keeping are included in the Annotated Bibliography.

The essence of the process is the bringing together of the particular combination of approaches which suit the needs of the individual. Here are some comments by an LEA assistant education officer about keeping a journal (a fuller version of the text is given in Chapter Six):

> "I have ... used the journal as an aid to a fairly specific programme of self development ... to build up strategies and to affirm progress and to try to understand and accept lack of it... I have ... found the journal to provide a wealth of clarity about events and interconnections, a depth of focus about my own and other people's value judgements".

References

HAMILTON, E 1985 *Professional partners* Publicity brochure Columbia, Maryland: Hamilton Associates

HERON, J 1981 'Self and peer assessment' in T Boydell and M. Pedler (eds) *Management self development: concepts and practices* Farnborough: Gower

CHAPTER FOUR
Support for Corporate Action

Here we are concerned with support in those circumstances where more complex changes in school management are being considered. There have been many studies of the process of planned change and a whole academic field has developed around the question of school review and curriculum evaluation. In recent years, several procedures have been developed to guide the process of school review and development: the Schools Council has produced guidelines for review and institutional development in schools (GRIDS, see McMahon et al 1984); many local education authorities have adopted instruments for school self-review. This is complemented by the experience in industry, where some major firms have developed detailed training manuals concerning the process of planned change. Something of this kind should be made readily available to all schools as an important source of support in introducing corporate change in school management. We refer in passing to these schemes to make the point that support for corporate action should be placed quite clearly within a systematic approach to school review and development.

Even with clear guidelines of this kind, there will be occasions when the head, who inevitably has a key role in any attempt at major change within the school, will welcome additional personal support. We give details of three types of activity, together with a consideration of schemes for cascade training. Further sources of information are listed in the Annotated Bibliography.

The Action Learning Set

The action learning set is a form of mutual support group for those intent upon solving a difficult or complex organisational problem.

The set usually consists of between five and seven members who may be drawn from different professional backgrounds and perhaps work for different organisations. The set holds one day meetings about every six weeks, often continuing to meet for a year or more in order to see through the various problems presented by the members.

After initial briefing, each member brings to the first meeting a real management problem encountered at work. Examples of problems addressed by secondary heads have included the introduction of a staff development policy in the school and the restructuring of the school day. Each session is devoted to an examination by the group of each problem in turn. As each individual reports, the other members of the group concentrate on insightful questioning in order to help clarify the nature of the problem, its origin and its causes. This leads to each set member identifying the action to be taken before the next session.

At the heart of the action learning set is the commitment to action, both in specifying and carrying out solutions to problems, coupled with a determination to continue meeting until all the problems have been solved. Obviously an openness to new perspectives and a combination of mutual trust and some stringency are essential to provide that blend of support and challenge likely to lead to personal development and effective action.

The set usually includes an adviser whose main role is to convene but not direct the set. The adviser also facilitates the process of reporting, questioning and analysing through which the set members support each other but does not engage directly in the task.

The Value of Action Learning

Over the past ten years, action learning has gradually become accepted as a method of management development in industry, commerce and the public sector. In most cases it is used as an alternative rather than as an aid to training courses. However, there are some industrial examples of its use in conjunction with more traditional courses (Casey, 1980). The project has had access to two attempts to incorporate the method within twenty day basic courses for secondary heads (Bristol and Sussex). At Sussex it was intended in part as a bridging activity which might be expected to continue after the formal course had ended.

The concept of action learning is powerful because of its simplicity. But its operation requires a full and sensitive appreciation of the processes of learning and support which are essential to the success of the set. There are additional difficulties encountered in using action learning sets in conjunction with more traditional training methods. To some extent this explains why, so far, its use by headteachers has had mixed success. This issue will be discussed later in this section.

Nevertheless, the potential of action learning is perhaps greater than any other activity, since the main function of the action learning set is to help managers integrate personal development with the practical issues of the working day. Despite all the difficulties, therefore, it merits careful examination in order to establish ways in which it can be adopted as a post-course activity. This is especially important in cases where the training experience has heightened the awareness of participants of the need for change, but has not made provision to support the consequent action.

The Process

The concept of action learning originated with Revans (1983) who has written prolifically on its development and application (see Annotated Bibliography). Revans makes a distinction between the acquisition of managerial skills and techniques (programme knowledge) and the ability to pose discriminating and insightful questions in conditions of ignorance, risk and confusion (questioning insight). Action learning occurs when the two are combined ($P + Q = L$). As each set fellow reports on the nature of the problem and progress made in grappling with it, the group members seek to clarify their understanding of the fellow's frame of reference and to probe its relevance. This may cause the fellow to reframe the problem before deciding on subsequent action. Exploring the problem, seeking advice and comment and deciding on action must be closely interlinked within the process.

As a result of his work with the Local Government Training Board, Harries (1981) has represented this process as a hierarchy of three activities: support/pressure, clarification, reporting.

The ratio between the three activities varies as the group develops in mutual confidence and ability:

Diagram 3: Development of Activities in an Action Learning Set (Harries, 1981)

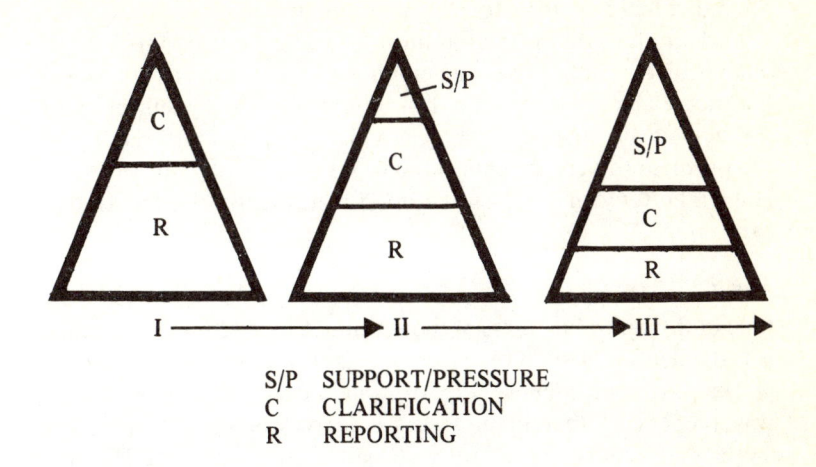

```
        I              II              III
       /\             /\              /\
      /C \          /S/P\           /S/P \
     /----\        /-----\         /------\
    /  R   \      /   C   \       /   C    \
   /--------\    /---------\     /----------\
                /     R     \   /     R      \
```

S/P	SUPPORT/PRESSURE
C	CLARIFICATION
R	REPORTING

A clear understanding of the process is helpful to members of an action set. In addition to the factors Harries outlines there are two others which are critical to the success of the set in achieving practical impact on the organisation:

The nature of the problem

This must above all be a real problem or opportunity facing the organisation and significantly affecting its future. It needs to be sufficiently complex to warrant serious and systematic exploration through an action set. Revans makes the distinction between problems (with no certain solution available) and puzzles (which can be solved simply by applying technical knowledge).

Solving a problem of this kind will involve a careful examination not only of its technical aspects but the conflicting responses to it by colleagues in the organisation and the underlying attitudes and values which may need to change if a solution is to be found and implemented.

The quality of the questioning

This has a twofold effect. Firstly set fellows must realise that the opportunity to 'get inside' another fellow's problem by exploring the frame of reference adopted, and to develop insights into alternative frameworks through which it might be perceived, is in itself a valuable learning experience. Secondly the quality of this insightful questioning is crucial to the support the group can offer the individual in getting to grips with the problem.

A clear and firm distinction must be made between this kind of analytical but supportive questioning and the kind of rhetorical questions which stem from a desire to proffer the benefit of one's own technical knowledge. There is a place for this, at the request of the problem solver, since this kind of information may be of value. But it is better to arrange a separate, private meeting for this kind of exchange.

The Set Adviser

One of the central features of the action set as conceived by Revans was the demystification of learning. Experts are unnecessary to the working of a set; managers learn to help each other. However, it was recognised that in most cases there would be a need for someone to convene the group at least. Some, including Revans, would query the need for any other form of assistance. The sets which operated as part of the Bristol course managed without set advisers.

Nevertheless, whilst the principle of mutual support by set members is generally accepted, there is a strong body of opinion that the person convening the set must, in the first instance, help the members to come to terms with the process. Braddick and Casey (1981) for example require the set adviser to ask 'meta questions' about how the task is being done and what people are feeling about the questioning that is taking place; the aim is to encourage a more rigorous exploration of the frame of reference being adopted in treating the problems. Others would expand the role of the set adviser to include the establishing of a personal contract with each member, encouraging or even supervising the individual tasks between meetings and keeping the group members in touch with a wider network. But there is a danger of confusing the role of set adviser with the personal responsibility of members to solve their problems and to seek technical advice if needed. The set adviser is not a teacher and if supervision of task achievement is needed it should be provided within the normal managerial structure of the organisation. In the last analysis it is best to keep the idea of action learning simple and direct; give the members a clear idea of the aims and methods of working and let them get on with the job.

Recruitment and Organisation

Recruitment is a difficult matter since active self-selection of participants is essential. Attempts to 'draft' members are almost certain to result in failure, especially in cases where heads are used to a large measure of autonomy in their working life. In order to give the degree of commitment necessary to the process, members must have a sound understanding of action learning before committing themselves to a set. It is useful therefore to make information available about action learning and to encourage informal discussion of its merits well in advance of any opportunity to become involved. Some would advocate a special familiarisation course of a day or two.

The range of managerial experience of the set

Balancing the set membership is another important factor. Members might be drawn deliberately from very different backgrounds and organisations in order to ensure that each problem will be perceived in many different ways. They may be from different sections of one large organisation in order to encourage a better understanding of the different parts.

The frequency of set meetings

This must relate sensibly to the amount of time allocated to the whole project and varies considerably from set to set. If members are working full time on the problems, then a weekly meeting may be necessary. But if the work has to be fitted into the normal load, more time will be needed between meetings for action to be implemented. There is some evidence that frequency of meeting correlates with task achievement, but this may simply relate to the amount of time available and the demands of other duties.

The duration of meetings

Meetings must be long enough to allow the proper consideration of each project. Each member must have time to make a full progress report and to be questioned by the others. A whole day needs to be set aside for most meetings.

Personal contracts

Proper working briefs are essential if a practical project is to be pursued. The creation of this contract is not the responsibility of the set or the set adviser. It rests between the individual member and colleagues in the organisation. However, the proceedings of the set will no doubt lead each member to seek a redefinition of the contract with colleagues as the problem is reframed and a plan of action emerges.

Difficulties to be Overcome

Action learning has something to offer to headteachers in its own right, without any connection with training courses, providing it is set in the broader framework of management development. We have more to say on this issue in Chapter Five. However our concern here is with the provision of support for heads undergoing the training currently available to them. We have already indicated that there are difficulties in using action learning in this way, but the need to offer practical support in converting the results of training into action outweighs them.

Any attempt to provide action learning requires a sound appreciation of its procedures coupled with a careful assessment of the difficulties encountered. The previous section summarised the main aspects of process and organisation. Here we will list some of the difficulties before suggesting three possible lines of action.

Action learning seen as a course

There is a danger of confusing action learning with traditional course provision. Generally speaking, people who go on courses expect to learn about things; they expect knowledge to be transferred efficiently from someone else to them. Action learning is organised in the face of these expectations; the individual must be committed to tackle a problem, learn from experience and open the mind to new approaches to old situations. But there are many conventional attitudes which implicitly undermine this. Apart from the members' expectations of training, trainers too have conventions and expectations. As action learning has gained in popularity, programmes have been designed and marketed; 'experts' have emerged and seek to recruit people to fill up their action sets. To some extent these functions are necessary, but it is all too easy for the pendulum to swing too far and the spirit and purpose of action learning to disappear. What transpires is a 'contrived action learning programme with many of the faults of any training package' (Casey, 1980).

There are extra dangers where action learning is associated

directly with more conventional courses. Even where members are informed in advance that the course will include action learning sessions, these are still likely to be regarded as just another module in the course. Consequently, the level of commitment to action learning will vary from individual to individual; problems will be produced because it is a requirement of the course and not for their significance to the school.

Single profession sets

Headteachers are too familiar with each other's situation. The benefits of action learning sets are the variety of perspectives offered by its members and the "fresh look" at each situation. This is difficult to achieve with a group of heads. It is difficult for them to avoid slipping into comparative anecdote and general discussion of the state of their schools. Where set members come from the same LEA, they are often reluctant to speak freely and openly about their problems.

Set advisers

The role of the set adviser is difficult to combine with other supporting functions . Where action learning sets are linked to courses, trainers or tutors may double up as set advisers. There are difficulties here since the roles may be in conflict and the switch difficult to effect without causing confusion or undermining the purpose of the set. Similarly if LEA advisers or officers act as set advisers there may be role conflict of a different kind.

Time allocation

Heads find it hard to allocate adequate time and stick to this allocation. Everyone has problems finding time for activities outside the normal routine, however important they are. But most people engaging in action learning do so within a clear framework set by an immediate superior. This will not be the case with heads who will usually have to make their own framework. Far too frequently the only time they allocate specifically is for attending set meetings. Even then in our experience other duties or unexpected crises can lead to a high absence rate. Absence from set meetings and lack of effective action by individuals between meetings have a negative effect on the rest of the set.

Three Possible Lines of Action

Each of the problems mentioned above is serious, but in combination they can create an 'anti-action syndrome'. Consequently any provision for action learning must attempt to offset them in some way. There appear to be three possibilities:

Single profession sets

Despite the inherent problems, sets for headteachers alone still offer one way of proceeding. Moreover it has the advantage of providing an easy way to create sets for all those members of training courses who express some interest in continuing to focus on school problems beyond the course. The previous shared experience of the members has some advantages for the set. However, it will still need very careful recruitment linked to the debriefing procedures of the training course. Indeed, if provision of action learning is planned it is helpful if discussions about possible membership can begin in the initial briefing sessions before the course and continue throughout – leaving the final decision on membership of a set until much later. Success will also depend on careful time budgeting. Although the head will remain responsible for this, it is important for the authority in providing the opportunity to negotiate an appropriate commitment. The question of an appropriate set adviser has been raised and remains to be resolved.

Multi-professional sets

involving managers from industry and commerce offer distinct attractions. The difficulty is in finding a suitable method of recruiting enough sets to meet the needs of all interested heads. Provision within the private sector tends to be more expensive than LEAs are used to. However by planning ahead it should be possible to arrange for local collaboration. Membership of sets by LEA officers and advisers (not as set advisers) has much to recommend it. It broadens out the perspectives of the set and provides a valuable experience in partnership with heads.

Integrated sets

that is sets operating within formal training courses, have already been attempted in the twenty day basic courses at Bristol and Sussex. The outcome of the first round of courses has been mixed,

with the Bristol course reporting the better results. Reports of the Bristol and Sussex experiments are set out in Chapter Six. The following points emerge from the Bristol experiment:
- many members can make useful progress with problems in their own jobs using this method;
- the group is a valuable aid for analysing problems, generating solutions, giving confidence and support;
- a minority has difficulties in handling the method;
- more have difficulty selecting appropriate problems to tackle;
- others found their efforts inhibited by industrial action in the schools;
- perspectives are usefully broadened and assumptions challenged when sets include LEA officers and advisers (who are also full members of the twenty day course at Bristol);
- sets have a limited life and do not transform into permanent organisations.

The Sussex sets were deliberately scheduled at the end of the formal course so that members might respond to problems and opportunities which emerged during the year and were perceived more clearly as a result of the training experience. The three course modules took place between January and May. Five full days were allocated to action learning between May and September. Members of the earlier OTTO course acted as set advisers, themselves advised by an experienced action learning consultant.

This plan was presented to the members at the beginning of the course, but not raised again formally until April at a one day introductory session led by the consultant and a manager from industry who had used action learning.

In summer 1984 schools were disrupted by industrial action and heads were preoccupied with this problem (although strangely none saw this as an appropriate topic for the action learning set). This preoccupation accounts, to a large extent, for the lack of progress made by many members. But the location of the sets at the end of the course, yet still as part of it, may have been a problem. The inexperience of the set advisers (despite consultant's support) may also have created some confusion.

The lessons to be learnt seem to be:
- if action learning is to be integrated within a twenty day course it must be perceived by members as central to the whole course and not peripheral;

- support for sets is better left at the simple administrative level rather than creating complex adviser roles without suitable personnel (providing set members have a clear understanding of their brief);
- sets must have a sufficient life-span to allow each member to settle on a genuine and worthwhile problem. This is unlikely to be achieved at the first attempt;
- a mixed set of LEA officers and heads is an advantage.

External Consultancy

The basic idea of help from an external consultant in implementing corporate change seems quite sound. Consultancy is widely used by industrial and commmercial management as well as in other parts of the public sector, but it is seldom encountered in any direct form in schools. Although advisers may perform a consultancy function in certain technical areas (e.g. curriculum specialisms and teacher selection), they operate less frequently in broader areas of corporate change.

Explanations can be offered for the absence of consultants from schools:
- it is difficult to locate appropriate consultancy skills at a price schools can afford.
- consultancy is a professional relationship which is regulated by the client exercising choice in selecting the consultant; the resource structure in education does not give schools the scope to do this.
- consultancy is labour intensive at a high level of professional operation; education tends to lock up its major recurrent resource in permanent appointments.
- schools are public bodies with publicly controlled policies; in questions of corporate action it is sometimes difficult to determine who in the school should be the client (head, staff or governors).

Nevertheless, in drawing up the Joint Plan, it is worth considering what kinds of consultancy it might be useful to make available in support of corporate action and where consultants might be located at a feasible cost.

Types of consultancy function

Consultants come in many forms but it is useful to distinguish

three categories in relation to support for school management:
- advice on technical management skills (e.g. financial systems, curriculum design).
- advice on personal relations (e.g. management style, communication skills).
- advice on the process of planned change.

The third category is more directly related to corporate action and is our major concern here. To some extent the first two categories relate more to personal action and have been covered briefly in the previous section on mutual support groups. However they must also be taken into account as elements within the process of planned change.

Support for the process of planned change

Perhaps the most useful study of support for planned change was produced by Havelock (1973). He argued the need for "change agents". Havelock derived their functions from a synthesis of various approaches to planned change: a problem solving process where the client needs help with the analysis of the problem and access to external resources (knowledge, ideas etc.) in the search for a solution and in the attempt to implement it. Help, according to Havelock, could be provided through a series of inter-linked roles, of which the following are of interest in this context:
- Catalyst: applying some indirect pressure to overcome complacency and to start working on serious problems.
- Solution giver: finding workable solutions and helping with their adaptation to the particular needs of the school.
- Process helper: advising on the complex and vulnerable process of planned change.
- Resource linker: bringing together diagnostic skills, solutions, people, time and energy to effect planned change.
- Evaluator: providing insights into the consequences of attempts to change, the various perceptions of the people involved and the effectiveness of the outcomes.

Sources of support

It should be possible for LEAs and providers to make arrangements through the Joint Plan to offer some limited support for some of these functions on a selective basis. Possible sources of support which might be considered are:
- the advisers and officers are often placed in the position of

catalyst, and in specialist areas may act as solution givers; but advisers or area officers alone are in a position to act as resource linker and this must be seen as their key role.
- higher education staff on a selective basis can offer assistance with solutions and with the process; but they are likely to serve best as evaluators.
- the consultant head is likely to be of best use as solution giver or process helper.
- colleague heads can offer support in all functions (except perhaps resource linker) through inter-visitations; these are similar in organisation to the professional partnerships described in the previous section.
- industrial personnel should not be discounted as potential consultants, particularly on process; there are frequent occasions when a firm's own management development programme will make such arrangements of mutual benefit.

It would seem from this brief survey that no one source of consultancy is sufficient to offer a full range of support. On the other hand, heads will probably not need consultant support in all aspects. However, it is quite feasible for the authorities, in drawing up the Joint Plan with the providers, to consider what local resource can be made available to heads planning to undertake complex corporate change.

LEA Task Groups

The requirements for corporate action can sometimes be wider than the single school. Increasingly there is the need for collaboration and coordination between schools. Examples might include a local scheme of school reorganisation or the development of a consortium solution to problems of curriculum provision. Training programmes do not usually relate directly to such circumstances, but management training can have a positive influence providing it is planned and organised to do so.

Where the need for a task group has been established in advance of training this will require some adjustment in course provision to take account of the requirements of the task group members. Indeed, the one term training opportunity (OTTO) is particularly well suited to these circumstances. But there will also be occasions where the need for a task group emerges during debriefing. An example is given under cascade training, where several heads seek to collaborate in staff development provision. Training might in this case be seen as a preliminary to the task, providing heads with a general preparation or simply heightening awareness of the issues involved. Consequently, in establishing the Joint Plan, LEA and provider should consider the possibility of task groups following on from training.

The need for collaboration and coordination at the area level is clear as LEAs seek to maintain the service in increasingly difficult circumstances and, at the same time, make a planned response to requests for new courses and curricula.

However it is important to note that there are two kinds of group:
- representative groups, where heads are convened to work on a problem on behalf of a wider group of schools, or on aspects of general education policy;
- mutual groups, where all the schools concerned are fully involved in the process, together with officers responsible for related services.

Heads taking OTTO fellowships sometimes hold a brief to develop LEA policy on a "representative" basis, but for the most part we expect opportunities for mutual task groups to be more common. In Chapter Five we give examples of training which is specifically geared to the needs of a mutual task group. Here we are concerned with task groups associated with more general forms of training.

The Process

Whatever the nature of the problem, steps must be taken to ensure that the group is clearly established as a *task* group and has the conditions necessary to achieve its objects. There are several points worth listing if only to provide a check list for consideration at the time of formulating the Joint Plan.

Climate and image

The purpose of the group is to achieve coordinated action. This sense of purpose will be reinforced or undermined by the nature of the arrangements the authority is seen to make in support of the exercise. It may be pedantic to make a distinction between a task group and a working party, but success requires much more than the submission of a report. The members of the group need to be committed to implementing their plan of action. They must have confidence in the support of the authority in their work.

The concept of an initial planning brief

It is helpful, in guiding the task, to prepare a formal statement of terms of reference and the reporting relationships of the group. In addition, the factors mentioned below need to be discussed with the group members and clarified before work begins. This initial brief will need to be renegotiated as work proceeds.

Support services

The task group needs to be properly organised with a secretariat and an information service. It may be that the members themselves must take on the duties, but separate provision sharpens the sense of task and has a marked effect on morale. It may well be that these are functions which the convenor should be responsible for providing.

Timescale

It is important that some estimate of the lifespan of the group is made; widely differing expectations can cause confusion.

Budget

The most important consideration is the question of time allocated to the task. This may not involve replacement teaching since the work is a part of headship, but it will require a specific commitment of time both for meetings and for action between meetings.

A small materials and travel budget may also be needed. It heightens the sense of purpose if the budget is clearly within the control of the group; there is a distinction between a group budget and ad hoc allocations from the general training budget.

Officer and Adviser Involvement

We have not looked to increase dependence upon advisers and officers in our suggestions for support, since it is generally acknowledged that time is their scarce resource. However in these circumstances it would seem to be highly appropriate for an officer to convene the group. The basis of the task group as described here is that LEA involvement is necessary to develop and implement solutions. It follows from this that if real and difficult problems are to be addressed by the group, then the officer or adviser involved must have sufficient authority (by position or specific brief) to facilitate action. This has considerable implications in drawing up the relevant details of the Joint Plan. For example, in an authority where responsibility for the Joint Plan rests with a senior adviser, consultation with area officers will be necessary where their general responsibilities make them the proper choice to act as convenors.

Cascade Training

Heads returning from a management training experience may be willing to provide training for others. There are many examples of heads providing courses for deputies and heads of department and this provides a valuable added training resource for the LEA. However it will often be sensible for the head to concentrate first on implementing the results of training before turning to the problems of further dissemination.

Nevertheless, there are specific instances where 'cascade' training is a necessary preliminary to the introduction of new management practice in the school. For example, many training modules on management style require the concepts and techniques to be acquired by colleagues before they can be implemented. Moreover, the introduction of well conceived management training programmes at the school level is part of the management task of the head. Consequently, it is important to consider ways of supporting further training at the school level. The National Development Centre is producing guidelines for the management development process in schools. Our concern here is to focus on the school's capacity to locate or provide training experiences which are an essential part of such a system.

Support is especially important in those cases where, perhaps as a result of ideas encountered in training, a head wishes to go beyond the provision of a single course and is taking steps to set up a planned programme of management training in the school. In such cases it is important to link the provision of training directly with the school's educational policies and management practices. We describe here some of the factors which must be taken into account in the organisation and development of training programmes at the school level.

Such a programme will make use of a wide variety of training opportunities, many of which will be provided at LEA or regional level. However, if the school is to ensure that the programme is fully integrated within the broader requirements for staff and policy development, some measure of independently initiated training will be necessary. This specially targeted training can be provided either in-house or for a few local schools sharing the same needs. However an integrated programme will only be achieved if the head has a clear oversight of its development, although the level of personal involvement might vary considerably. On the other hand, it is unreasonable to expect schools to undertake such a programme unaided. Some external input in terms of both funding and specialist personnel will be necessary to help them achieve an appropriate quality of training experience.

We wish to examine the organisational arrangements which can be made to bring together these various factors and enable an effective school-focussed training programme to be developed. Although there is a good deal of overlap between the various possibilities, it is convenient to consider them separately under three headings:

- in-house programmes (for one school);
- the cluster group (a few schools collaborating);
- the local course initiated by the LEA (focussing on special policy issues).

Each of these will be described briefly, although the nature of each exercise is fairly obvious from the name.

The provision of training requires more than an organisational framework. One cannot overemphasise the importance of the development process if the training is to be effective. Far too often, courses are organised rather than developed; topics are listed, speakers enlisted and the course is run. There are important issues relating to the design of effective training experiences which must be taken into account. Since these are common to to all the organisational forms they are considered separately.

Forms of Organisation

In-house training

A head's first concern in 'cascade' training is for the school and the staff, rather than any wider LEA training needs. Consequently the place to begin is in the school. The first and greatest advantage of in-house training is that it can be directly linked to the wider question of management development. Training experiences can be developed in response to the specific needs perceived within the school to improve the school management function. The further one moves away from the school in selecting training opportunities for the staff, the greater the chance that they will not be quite what is wanted. If a school is able to provide its own training it can lower the barrier between school and course and link the experience directly to the daily working routine.

However, locating training in the school does not in itself ensure relevance. Fostering enthusiasm and achieving an effective linkage with management practice in the school will require quite deliberate departures from the traditional modes of training. Basing training in the school makes this more feasible. For example, one can rely less on visiting speakers, artificial case studies and simulations and spend more time on exercises and investigations based directly on the life and work of the school. These types of individual and small group activity can sometimes be fitted into personal timetables, taking the emphasis away from day closures and the consequent need to provide activities for the whole staff.

In-house training also makes it possible to focus on teams in an attempt to improve the ability of staff to work together in year groups, departments or in the senior management team. The aim should be to encourage teams to see training and development as an integral part of their working life and necessary to their proper functioning. Like any other aspect of their work they might expect to take an active part in its planning.

All this needs time and resource. It may be possible to mount the occasional training activity as a special event without too much effort; but a move towards team training and systematic management development requires an adequate internal management structure and in itself calls for the application of management skills. These matters are dealt with further below.

The cluster group

One way of overcoming the restrictions of size which limit the scope of in-house training is to collaborate with other schools in cluster groups of about five or six. The opportunity to establish a cluster group may arise out of heads sharing a common management training experience. The target population will consist of about 300 teachers including twenty senior staff and perhaps sixty heads of department. This ensures viable groups in any one category of management training.

Other advantages include the ability to share the overall task of programme design, thus rendering training more cost effective. Moreover, the cluster group might be seen to constitute a significant training unit within the LEA, meriting the planned allocation of resources including adviser time.

However, there is some evidence that schools find collaboration at this level quite difficult to achieve. Although there are several experiments of this kind underway (notably in Cleveland and Dudley), it is too early to assess their effectiveness. Moreover, one should not underestimate the level of resource and expertise to be invested including professional time, course design skills and experience of adult learning strategies.

The local course

Although not directly related to the question of 'cascade' training, some local courses initiated by the LEA provide a valuable complement to it. This is especially true of those addressed to specific issues which schools face in common, providing an opportunity for heads or senior staff to assess the implications for school policy and management practice. The course gives schools a clearer understanding of external factors which are calling for change and helps them formulate an appropriate institutional response.

Examples of this kind of provision have been found in the following categories:
- as a response to a national initiative, such as changes in the public examination system or in specific curricular areas (e.g. GCSE, CPVE, TVEI);
- as a means of clarifying the response to a particular item of LEA policy (e.g. multi-ethnic education);
- as a response to technological innovation (e.g. information technology);
- as a response to a local situation (e.g. school amalgamation).

An alternative approach to the provision of this kind of support is suggested in the next section on LEA task groups.

The Organisation and Design of Effective Training Experiences

Whichever organisational form is adopted for the training programme, adequate arrangements must be made within the school to ensure that it is planned and organised effectively. Our chief concern is with the quality of course design and the imaginative use of a range of different types of activity. But if the training is to become an integral part of the school's approach to management, then it needs to be treated as a serious piece of planning and management in itself.

Several national projects in recent years have touched upon related issues and it is helpful to draw on their experience. Two Schools Council projects – *School-based Staff Development Activities* (see Oldroyd et al 1984) and *GRIDS* (see McMahon et al 1984) – offer useful advice on the type of planning process which will be needed. Of more direct relevance are the guidelines for management development in the secondary school which are being produced by the National Development Centre for School Management Training. These will soon be available to schools and authorities and will be of interest to those concerned with training and management development at the school level. Our purpose here is to summarise the main factors which must be taken into account. Clearly, the degree to which they are taken up will vary according to the size and complexity of the intended programme.

It is convenient to summarise the main points under five headings: securing support and approval, setting up a management structure, developing the programme, implementing the programme, evaluation.

Securing support and approval

Consult: clearly, if all that is envisaged is a single course, informal consultations with those to be involved will be all that is necessary. However, if a more substantial programme is intended, there will be a need for more systematic consultation – with the staff to ensure their involvement and with the LEA to secure assistance.

Create a climate: consultation will involve a series of discussions with various internal groups, especially those who might already be seen to be engaged in development activities and therefore likely to be pacemakers in any programme. Despite the staff's professional background, there are likely to be many differing views of the nature of mid-career professional training – not all of which will be positive. Formal consultation with the whole staff and with union representatives will be necessary at the appropriate stage.

Establish a policy: The formal presentation of the policy will include a description of the aims and purposes, the operating principles and the level of activity envisaged in the first phase.

Setting up a management structure

Allocate responsibility: the head will no doubt want to keep in close touch with developments, but most of the preparations will be delegated. The choice of coordinator is critical to the success of the programme. The advice of the School-based Staff Development Activities Project is 'use well respected, positive adaptable school leaders'. The coordinator will need enthusiasm, energy and administrative ability more than seniority.

Give the coordinator an initial planning brief: this will be developed from the policy statement and should include provisional details and levels of expectation on: the size of operation, timescale for implementation, budget for development and implementation (cash and time).

Renegotiate brief: the initial brief should be renegotiated in the light of subsequent experience. It then becomes a useful management tool for monitoring progress in an open and constructive way.

Developing the programme

Assess training needs: this requires careful consultation and collaboration with members of staff engaged in management duties to ascertain those aspects of management which might need to be changed or improved. The important point here is to ensure that the assessment is geared to management need and not just to the availability of training opportunities.

Settle on a training target for the first phase: this should not be too grand. The process of assessment will have provided an opportunity to identify those members of staff most likely to collaborate in the early stages of the programme. The aim should be to build upon this enthusiasm. Thus the programme will be somewhat opportunistic and piecemeal at this stage. The main criterion should be the quality and relevance of the experience. There will be opportunities later to cross-fertilise from the early successes.

Design the programme: teachers are already familiar with the procedures of curriculum design. However there are some points to be made about the design of mid-career training experiences:

- base activities on the notion of 'learning from experience' and not just on knowledge transfer. This means relying less on talks and discussions;
- use case studies and simulations if you find them helpful;

- investigations into school management practice, enquiries and planning exercises are much closer to the real task of trying to improve personal and collective management performance;
- encourage people to work in pairs or small groups and to plan their investigations as 'task teams', sharing out the various parts of the job;
- encourage teams to schedule this investigative work flexibly, with a balance of individual work and team meetings;
- arrange for visiting speakers where they fit into the work of the groups;
- remember that oral presentation followed by questions and discussion is not always the best way to explore new ideas or the most efficient use of time. Where specialist inputs are required, there is much to be gained from the discussion and analysis of prepared papers rather than relying entirely on oral presentations;
- provide administrative support for the teams in their work. If staff are expected to conduct investigations and surveys, they will benefit from a good information service which makes available extracts from relevant DES reports, LEA documents, professional journals and the press. This kind of support greatly enhances the climate in which the whole programme operates.

Implementing the programme

The operation of the programme very much depends on the details of its design. But certain principles are important to observe:
- the overall climate in which the programme is set is vital to its success and this depends very much on the attitude of the head and the coordinator towards it. The management of the programme must be seen by the staff as a service to their professional needs rather than a form of supervision;
- involvement in training activities must be given a clear priority rating alongside other duties;
- whilst most of the activities rely on self-help and are inexpensive (apart from staff time), they must be fully resourced if they are to be taken seriously;
- unless time and effort is allocated to the implementation of the outcomes of training, it will remain ineffective and rightly regarded as peripheral to the work of the school.

Evaluation

There is one important aspect concerning evaluation which needs to be clarified. Evaluation is often seen as a separate 'end process'. But it is more useful to see it as three functions, each integrated within the total programme:

- the first function of evaluation is to enable the programme to be adjusted as it runs, in order to ensure that its objects are achieved. Providing there has been adequate negotiation with the participants concerning the practical reasons for undertaking training, an interim evaluation can help to keep things on track. The concept of the initial brief referred to above can also be applied to the monitoring of the training experience;
- the second function is a natural continuation of the first and relates to the need to make adequate arrangements to ensure that what is gained from training can be evaluated for its potential for implementation by the individual, the team or the school as a whole. This process will also include a review of future training requirements;
- the third function is the more familiar one of assessing the usefulness of the training experience for future use with other people.

References

BRADDICK, B & CASEY, D 1981 'Developing the forgotten army – learning and the top manager' *Management Education and Development* Vol 12 Part 3 pp 169-180

CASEY, D 1980 'Transfer of learning – there are two separate problems' in J Beck and C Cox (eds) *Advances in management education* Chichester: Wiley

HARRIES, J 1981 'The role of action learning set advisers' *Training* Vol 7 No 2 pp7-8

HAVELOCK, R 1973 *The change agent's guide to innovation in education* New Jersey: Educational Technology Publications

McMAHON, A BOLAM, R ABBOTT, R and HOLLY, P 1984 *Guidelines for review and internal development in schools: secondary school handbook* York: Longman for the Schools Council

OLDROYD, D SMITH, K and LEE, J 1984 *School-based staff development activities: a handbook for secondary schools* York: Longman for the Schools Council

REVANS R 1983 'Action Learning: its terms and character' *Management Development* Vol 21 No 1 pp 39-50

CHAPTER FIVE

Developing New Forms of Training Opportunities to promote the Transition to Better Systems of Management Development

A major premise of this study is that the transition from the current forms of support for school management towards more comprehensive programmes of management development can best be achieved by planned incremental change. Immediate action to increase the effectiveness of existing training programmes by consolidating and coordinating arrangements for preparation and follow-up activities is an important first step. Recommendations in this area constitute our main brief and, in the previous chapters, we have concentrated on the practical details of the local Joint Plan necessary to achieve this. We now wish to examine the second part of the two-stage strategy of incremental development. We will make the case for a medium term policy of experimentation with different forms of training provision. Training experiences can be designed to connect training more directly to the issues and problems of school management which the heads encounter and, in some cases, to incorporate management action and management change within the training experience.

In some ways, this second stage of development is not a new departure but an extension of the action taken under the Joint Plan, and the case for experimentation needs to be made. To do this, we must first return to our initial premise that the transition to systems of management development is best achieved by planned incremental change. It is from our understanding of the nature of this transition that we consider new developments in training have an important contribution to make.

The Case for Incremental Change

There is a growing body of opinion which regards the establishment of comprehensive programmes of management development at LEA level as a first requirement. The opinion is backed by sound argument: effective management development involves a range of activities, on and off the job, to assess personal development needs in the context of the Authority's educational policies and programmes; training programmes are but one part of these activities and doubt is cast on their practical value in the absence of any systematic appraisal of personal and institutional development needs. We subscribe to this broader definition of management development and the role of training within it. However, in our opinion, there is scope over the next two or three years for several developments in training which will maintain the momentum established by the early phase of the national initiative in moving towards the long term goal of more integrated systems of management development.

The National Development Centre for School Management Training (NDC) has responded to the call for management development systems by establishing a pilot scheme with LEAs which is attempting to produce appropriate models and procedures. However, it is already clear that not all LEAs are ready for such a major change at this stage and would find it difficult to move quickly and easily to implement a comprehensive and effective programme.

This report correlates with the work of the NDC by examining the range of intermediate actions available to LEAs in moving to the position where fully fledged management development programmes are feasible. Support for school management should be developed incrementally over the next few years towards effective management development programmes.

The need for further incremental change is seen more clearly when the current situation is reviewed in the context of events as they have developed nationally over the last five or six years. In 1981, the Hughes Report outlined the opportunities available to senior staff in schools and colleges to further their professional development. As far as secondary heads were concerned, it revealed a very bleak picture. They took up very few of the secondments to award bearing courses and were poorly represented on the part-time variants, no doubt because the demands of part-time study conflicted with their duties in school. Non-award bearing provision was found to be 'patchy and uneven ... the disturbing impression gained is that in many areas the provision is fortuitous and unplanned'. Here too the Hughes Report, in its analysis of membership, showed that secondary heads were even less well provided for than other categories of management.

At about the time of the Hughes Report, several regional initiatives were taking shape. Already the authorities in the north west and the north east had organised themselves into consortia for management training provision; ILEA and Surrey had established their own secondary head training programmes. New consortia were emerging in Yorkshire and Humberside, the West Country and in Sussex. Many authorities and individual headteachers were establishing links with industrial training units. There was vigorous debate on the nature and organisation of training opportunities, but there was a growing body of opinion on the need for a more systematic approach.

The national initiative launched through the Department of Education and Science Circular 3/83 brought a timely injection of funds and a strong impetus towards a reconsideration of the scope and nature of management training. In the first two years over 2,400 teachers including 300 secondary heads have engaged in training. Perhaps more significant in the long term is the evidence of a growing awareness amongst heads, LEA officers and training institutions of the broader concept of management development. In many parts of the country there is now a far greater dialogue between the various partners in the provision of management training. There are also signs that the nature of the provision is beginning to change so that the training is focussed more directly and more purposefully upon the individual's experience of school management.

Thus, attempts to improve support for school management must be set in this context of incremental change. It is more than mere optimism to assume that we are in transition from the 'patchy and uneven provision' observed by Hughes towards the management development programmes envisaged by the NDC. But it would be a mistake to assume that the transition is completed. The climate has not yet been created within the profession to make an immediate move towards implementing management development systems. In raising the level of awareness, the national initiative may already have taken us a good deal of the way towards more effective systems of management development, but they still cannot be reached in a single step. The general increase in the level of awareness of management development issues needs to be consolidated and developed further.

This view of the current state of affairs is confirmed by the experience of the NDC in its study of the problems of transition to

Table 3: Possible Stages in the Adoption of a Management Development Approach by LEAs
(NDC Director's Report No. 4 1985)

Stage	Main Observable Features	No. of l.e.a.s
1	The l.e.a. makes little management training provision of any kind for heads and senior staff. Its use of external courses, including 4/84, is small.	A diminishing minority
2	The l.e.a. makes considerable use of internal and external courses but on an ad hoc basis and without any clear policy framework. This includes its use of 4/84 provision. It is only just becoming aware of the 'development' approach.	The majority
3	The l.e.a. has been working for several years on the evolution of a management training policy related to school improvement. (The pattern of activities is varied, vigorous and well established but still consists mainly of courses. Most heads and senior staff have experienced them and, occasionally, so too have officers and advisers. In consequence, there is a reasonably common understanding in the l.e.a. of the possibilities and limitations of training, including 4/84 provision, and, accordingly, of the need to adopt a 'development' approach.	A growing minority
4	The l.e.a. has a coherent and explicit policy for management development aimed at school improvement. Procedures and staff exist for implementing the policy in the form of a regular programme. The programme includes the use of job descriptions, development interviews and other methods of diagnosing needs at individual, school and l.e.a. levels, and a varied range of on-the-job, close-to-the-job and off-the-job activities. Off-the-job courses, including 4/84 provision, are one component in the programme and the l.e.a. has an infrastructure and personnel capable of supporting course participants during the preparatory and following stages, and of relating such courses to the identified needs of the l.e.a. and its schools. Heads, senior staff, advisers and officers regularly engage in the programme which is systematically monitored and evaluated in terms of school improvement.	None at present

management development. The NDC has attempted a clarification of the situation by suggesting a four stage process for LEAs in adopting a comprehensive approach to management development (Table 3).

In his Director's Report, Bolam clearly indicates the need for a careful and deliberate approach to the transition from stage 2 to stage 3: 'the evidence from the pilot LEAs and the regional conferences indicates that the quantitative move from stage 1 to stage 2 can be achieved relatively quickly but that the qualitative move to stage 3 takes several years since it depends upon the creation of a climate of opinion, practice and understanding which can only come about as a result of sustained experiences'.

If this is an accurate assessment of the situation, it is important to develop local policy in the medium term which, taking account of the current state of development, is designed to create the 'sustained experiences' which will achieve this change in climate.

The Transition to More Effective Management Development

The current twenty day basic minimum training experience is already making an important contribution to this process of transition. Through the familiar conventions of 'the in-service training course' it can respond to participants on their own terms and introduce them to the notion of more systematic personal and institutional development. Once these concepts have been considered and accepted in principle, the other supporting activities arranged through the Joint Plan are available to help with their practical application. Furthermore these meetings between heads, officers and advisers, arranged to discuss personal development needs and school policy requirements, are themselves examples of the 'sustained experience' which Bolam claims is necessary to achieve this qualitative shift. However, it is possible to go further than this by designing training which, as an integral part of the experience, helps people develop more effective working relationships. This latter option is the one we examine here.

In general, current training is undertaken with strangers, rather than people with whom the head normally comes into regular working contact. It is also perceived as an experience, related to but separate from the actuality of current policies and programmes. In both relationships and preoccupations it is designed to be 'once-removed' from the regular experience of headship. This is a perfectly acceptable form of training. A deliberate withdrawal from normal working conditions can help heads rethink their approach to school management and, with adequate preparations and arrangements for post-course support, can boost the normal, everyday process of professional development.

We are not arguing for a complete review of this form of training provision. However, from time to time opportunities occur to use training situations to help heads, sometimes with their school management team, sometimes with officers and advisers, to engage directly with important issues arising in educational planning and management within the school or at the local level. The special conditions of support which training provides can be used to help people develop new ways of working together to ensure an effective and well coordinated service. When the opportunity arises, training should forsake the vicarious experience of simulations, case studies and discussions of generalised issues in favour of straightforward work on the tasks of management which the participants need to address in their everyday work.

We are aware that many training courses already include various forms of project work and action learning exercises. But, if groups who work together under normal conditions can be recruited into training, and if steps are taken by senior officers to ensure that the tasks they undertake in training are real tasks which will have a bearing on future policies and programmes, then the training experience can have a major impact upon future working relationships. Effective post-course support is easier to provide since the training experience is not set apart from regular work in quite the same way as is usually the case. The new relationships it creates can be more easily sustained under normal working conditions.

In looking for opportunities to experiment with training of this kind, and taking the head as the central figure, we return to the distinction we made earlier between personal action relating to the head's own management performance and corporate action, where the head will need to work as part of a team. At the heart of effective management development and management action is the capacity of each individual to reflect intelligently upon the situations and to identify and achieve organisational objectives and solve problems effectively. Consequently, the dimension of personal development remains significant, and we offer one example of an experiment focussing directly on personal development. But, since the personal development of heads takes place in the context of the school and its educational purposes, the question of corporate action is, in our opinion, more significant. Here we would distinguish between those areas of management internal to the school where there is a need for a team approach and those which require close collaboration on an area or inter-school basis with officers, advisers and other heads.

Consequently, we identify three dimensions of school management which require attention: the dimension of personal development, the dimension of school development, the dimension of coordinated local development.

Although interconnected, each dimension represents a sphere of action involving different people and different types of management skills.

In each of these dimensions it is possible to create opportunities for development through the medium of the training experience as currently construed under the national initiative. We will consider each dimension separately and give examples of experiments currently under way. However, we do not offer these as models to be adopted by others. Many of them are at a very early stage of development and it is too soon to claim success; others have made only modest progress. We offer them merely as illustrations of the type of experimentation which is needed.

The Dimension of Personal Development

In previous chapters we have already made the point that personal development for heads is best seen in terms of "learning from experience". All experienced professionals must be prepared to see their own development in relation to the needs of organisational policies and to recognise that effective experiential learning of this kind requires a constant and systematic process which can all too easily be in conflict with the heavy routine demands of the working day. Thus, although there are heads who can manage their own development unaided, for most it is prudent from time to time to seek support at least to check that the process is as effective as it can be. For some, the needs will be greater. It is important to consider what form this support might take.

A good deal of attention has been paid to this question in recent years and the work of David Kolb has been most influential. Kolb describes experiential learning as a four-stage cycle (see Diagram 4).

Diagram 4: The Experiential Learning Model

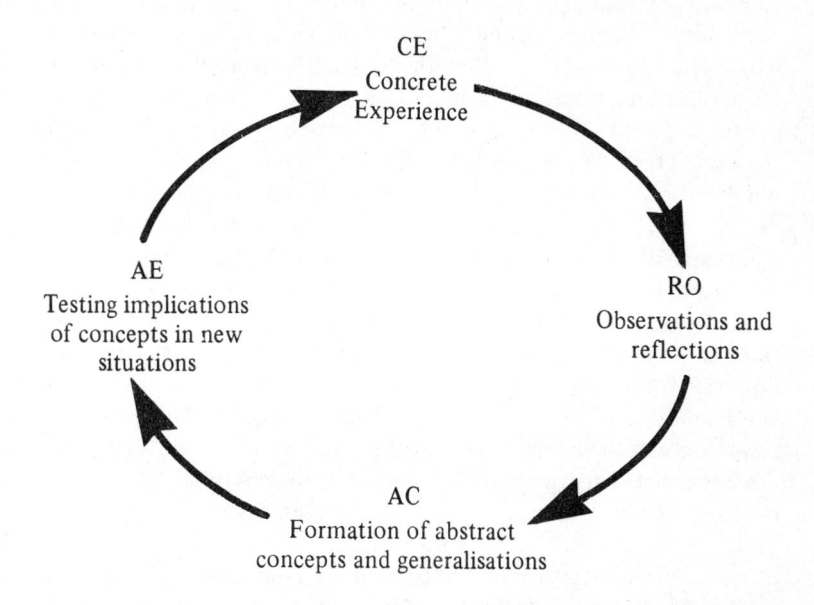

```
                    CE
                Concrete
                Experience


AE                                          RO
Testing implications              Observations and
of concepts in new                     reflections
   situations


                    AC
              Formation of abstract
           concepts and generalisations
```

'Immediate concrete experience is the basis for observation and reflection. These observations are assimilated into a 'theory' from which new implications for action can be deduced. These implications or hypotheses then serve as guides in acting to create new experiences' (1975 p.34).

Taken at face value this seems to be a straightforward account of an obvious logical process, but Kolb draws attention to the difficulties and conflicts inherent in any serious attempt to think and learn in this way. To be effective, the learner must operate on two dimensions, each containing polar opposites. The first is the concrete/abstract dimension which calls for the ability to remain open to new experience whilst at the same time being able to detach from it, grasp the whole and plan ahead. The second is the experimental/reflective dimension: the tension between active experimentation at one extreme and reflective observation at the other (p.36). Kolb then examines the different learning styles which people adopt in attempting to resolve these conflicts, showing that these vary quite markedly between individuals and may be inadequate to meet the demands of the working situation.

Kolb's work is firmly focussed on the function of experience in achieving growth and development. In this he is not alone. But his major contribution is in demonstrating that it is the use made of experience that matters: that the crucial issue is the process of learning from experience, not about it. This perspective must be contrasted with another, perhaps still dominant amongst heads and trainers. This sees the process of development in terms of satisfying needs, often expressed in terms of areas of skills and knowledge to be acquired (and, by implication, transmitted or discussed through training). We found several survey reports on this subject, often produced by seconded headteachers. As part of the process of management development each head will need to identify areas of skill and knowledge which will require further action, but the important first step is the ability to diagnose this need through a valid analysis of the experience of headship. Needs analysis is clearly a subordinate part of the process of learning and development. The question is how do heads continue to respond positively and effectively to the changing experience and challenge of headship? An over-concern for mapping generalised categories of need can deflect attention from the personal responsibility of each head to make and remake an individual assessment of need. It avoids the crucial question of the process by which this responsibility is discharged.

In considering the types of training experience which might aid this process of personal development we would draw attention to several of the activities recommended as support for personal action under the Joint Plan. In considering the elements of the Joint Plan, we were concerned to help convert the short term experience of development gained from training into a continuing process. Some of the activities proposed there would form the basis of experiment. The management self development workshop is especially relevant and is quite capable of being organised as an independent training experience. Full details are provided in Chapter Three. We are also aware that, because personal development must be closely linked with organisational development, it is often convenient for it to be subsumed within broader training programmes. Our recommendations in Chapter Two concerning personal contracts provide one method of achieving this. In addition, the following example drawn from recent industrial management training might also be of interest.

Richardson and Bennett of Roffey Park Management College,

supported by MSC funding, have recently experimented with industrial management training programmes drawing directly on Kolb's concepts of the learning cycle and individual learning styles.The experiment is described in detail in the Journal of European Management Training (Vol.8) but a short summary will be useful.

Richardson and Bennett (1984) note that a significant proportion of the needs which a manager must identify and satisfy are derived from an understanding of organisational policy. Personal development therefore relates to a capacity to identify and achieve organisational objectives and solve problems effectively. However, some managers find difficulty in developing these capacities because their preferred learning styles are inappropriate for the task.

They designed a four stage training programme to help managers assess the effectiveness of their learning style in dealing with the actual situations they faced at work.

- Stage One took place at work. The participant and his immediate superior worked together to complete a self-assessment questionnaire and to identify aspects of current performance which the participant would wish to strengthen.
- Stage Two took place at Roffey Park and presented the concept of preferred learning styles. The participants were then made aware of the ways in which they were able in everyday transactions to deny or 'discount' their ability or responsibilty for solving problems. Then, working in small groups, individuals produced action plans to meet their needs (solve the problems) identified on the job. In doing this, they were encouraged to adopt a more balanced learning style.
- Stage Three required the participants to implement the action plan back on the job, drawing in their immediate superior to discuss and agree organisational support for the plan.
- Stage Four took place six weeks later when participants met to review the whole learning process. The expressed wish of the organisers was that each would leave the review session with two planned areas of activity: a modification of the original action plan and, more importantly, an action plan for future learning and development for themselves and their subordinates.

This single cycle of supported personal development would seem to be too short to have long term significant effect. However this type of support is designed to help the manager develop more effective personal skills in the process of self development. Richardson and Bennett would also claim that it brings the manager and his colleagues into the kinds of relationships and experiences of joint action which are fundamental to the processes of management development.

The Dimension of School Development

The previous example demonstrates clearly that, even where the main concern is with personal development, an emphasis on learning from experience can only be achieved in the context of problems and issues current in the school. In training programmes, a shift of emphasis between personal development and school development is a matter of degree. We offer three examples of training programmes which show the nature of this shift. In the first, the Swedish national programme, the primary focus would still appear to be on the individual head, but the structure, content and timescale of the programme puts a much heavier emphasis on systematic attempts at school development than the example given in the previous section. In the second example, taken from the North-West Educational Management Centre programme, the starting point for training is the recognition of the need for schools in one urban authority to respond to the problems and opportunities created by a recent reorganisation of secondary schools. The third example is taken from our own work with two Surrey schools. Although this was a very small experiment, less well developed than the others, it allowed us to explore the important question of team development inside the school.

In Sweden there is a compulsory training programme for all school leaders (see for example Buckley 1985). It is a well established programme, developed in great detail by a national directorate supported by regional teams. However, a brief summary of its general features is sufficient here.

The programme comprises twenty-five days of residence divided into eight sessions of two to four days. These sessions are spread over two years to allow time for work back in the school. The aim of the programme is to integrate the personal development of each participant with a review of the work of their school and their role as school leader.

Most of the work back in the school over the two year period consists of observation, analysis and development work carried out with colleagues in school. The main purpose of the residential sessions is to review progress and plan further action. The school leader is expected to devote ten per cent of school time to this work and cover is provided.

Each school leader also undertakes four weeks of practical 'society-orientated' work in the locality: two weeks with social agencies and two weeks in industry or commerce.

The North-West Educational Management Centre working with the City of Liverpool provides the second example. The deliberate emphasis on school development is best demonstrated by the following extract from the document introducing the training experience to the heads:

> In September 1985 Liverpool will complete a major reorganisation of its County secondary sector which will reduce 24 schools to 16 and involve the closure of all the schools and reappointment of all 1,400 teachers in that sector. This follows a similar exercise in the Roman Catholic sector in 1983 when 41 schools, grammar and modern, were closed and 15 new comprehensive schools were opened, again with a major redistribution of staff. All 33 schools therefore face or have faced major challenges of integration and development.
>
> The North-West Educational Management Centre has agreed in principle, to a request from the Liverpool Education Authority to mount a twenty day course for about 30 Merseyside headteachers to study and make recommendations on school development in the post-reorganisation situation to operate during the academic year 1985-86...
>
> The programme would avoid the more traditional lecture-type input and would concentrate largely on action learning programmes with the participants identifying the problems and proposing the solutions.
>
> There will be plenary sessions addressed to some of the major topics and issues surrounding reorganisation but for the most part, participating heads will work in small planning groups of five or six to engage in real (not simulated) planning tasks directly related to the development of their own school. It is hoped to engage in one planning cycle during the Autumn term followed by a review in January, repeating the process in the second and third term of the year. Each group will have

considerable flexibility in devising its own timetable of meetings and venues.

An outside tutor would work with each group and the team of tutors would meet regularly under the guidance of NWEMC to assess progress and plan developments. There is a possibility, still to be discussed, that a manager from industry or commerce at a comparable level should be invited as a member of each of the groups....

It must be stressed that although this activity is being funded under the DES Management Training Scheme it cannot be seen as a course operating in isolation. It is the first phase of the school development programme outlined above. All its activities are geared to this end.

Notwithstanding the self-directed approach mentioned above, the overall programme for the course may well concern itself with the particular problems of post-reorganisational management which might include the following:

The period of stabilisation:
identify the needs of groups involved – pupils, parents, staff, community at large.

Prepare appropriate responses to anxieties, aspirations, motivation, defence and wrecking mechanisms of the groups so identified.

Organisation problems of amalgamations:
curriculum and timetable;
school organisation;
standards/level of expectation – work/behaviour;
pupil welfare – social and academic;
assessment and recording;
consultation procedures – pupils, parents, staff.

Directional development:
assessment of strengths;
analysis of previous practice;
diagnosis of needs;
consultation and decision making;
management of change.

School improvement programme:
to study individual schools' approaches to self evaluation and

school development. Existing programmes or models can be utilised as part of the study but it is expected that the exercises will be practical and experimental. Areas of study could include those in which some reorganised schools attempt to change an unfavourable image, or others seek to improve performance in public examinations, or develop a new role in the community which the school serves, or simply bring about major changes in the curriculum and organisation of the school. The existing work in this field, either the Schools Council/ SCDC GRIDS Project or the OECD School Improvement Project could be relevant and helpful...

The reference in this description to 'action learning programmes' is not unique. Several courses mounted under the national initiative adopt this approach for at least part of the programme. The significant difference here is that the action is clearly located within the authority's educational plans:

'this activity ... cannot be seen as a course operating in isolation. It is the first phase of the school development programme outlined above'.

It is also significant that the programme was presented to the heads in this context by the Director of Education as a genuine (not simulated) development task.

These two examples, although concerned with school development, have focussed on the head as the key figure in the process. Yet in both, there is a requirement to work with colleagues in the school. The kinds of in-school planning and review which these training experiences encourage will themselves need careful thought, since they will place new demands on the staff – especially those with senior management responsibilities. But these demands are not a product of the training experience, but of the environment in which most schools now find themselves. Schools are having to cope with external pressures for change on an increasing scale and often at quite short notice. Requirements to reorganise, to devise new curriculum packages, to prepare for new examinations, to respond to new policies such as multi-cultural education and children with special needs, are all current concerns in many schools. In order to cope successfully with these conditions, the 'senior management group' in the school will need to re-examine its working relationships.

These conditions of change and uncertainty are similar to those described by Burns (1963) in his study of the electronics industry. His analysis revealed the need to move to an 'organismic' pattern of working relationships in order to respond positively and effectively to the opportunities available in this environment:

'Organismic systems are adapted to unstable conditions, when new and unfamiliar problems and requirements continually arise which cannot be broken down and distributed among specialist roles within a hierarchy. Jobs lose much of their formal definition. The definitive and enduring demarcation of functions becomes impossible. Responsibilities and functions, and even methods and powers, have to be constantly redefined through interaction with others participating in common tasks or in the solution of common problems. Each individual has to do his job with knowledge of overall purpose and situation of the company as a whole'.

Internal support for school management groups in their attempts to review and develop their organisational structures can be made available through training experiences. There are many aspects of planning and organisation which internal management groups might profitably consider in group training. The most useful focus is a review of their own pattern of work set against their perceptions of the school's educational goals and in particular the ways in which they reorganise as a team to deal with new demands and opportunities.

As with training in personal development, attempts to experiment with this type of support will derive many insights from experiential group psychology. Whereas Kolb provides a focal point for individual development, Argyris and Schon (1974) provide a starting point for the process of team development. In common with Kolb, Argyris and Schon conclude that practice in administration and the professions is related to the competence of practitioners in taking action and simultaneously reflecting on this action to learn from it. They assume that all 'deliberate human behaviour' is determined by 'theories of action' developed and applied by the individual concerned. Professional effectiveness consists of acquiring, using and modifying appropriate theories of action. It is the quality of these 'theories in use' that governs successful practice in a complex and changing environment. In a later work, Argyris and Schon (1978) extend the concept of theories of action to the organisation itself:

'Organisations themselves are theories of action – theories of action which are maintained and transformed by individuals who occupy roles within organisational structures and live in the world draped over these structures' (preface).

The process of school development, therefore, should not be seen simply as the definition of new policies and programmes or as problem solving within the school's organisational system. It must take into account this reflexive dimension. Those with management responsibilities must be prepared to re-examine their assumptions about the best ways of working together, to test them against changing educational conditions and requirements, and to re-cast their roles and responsibilities in response to the review. Argyris and Schon shed light on the group interactions that are necessary in moving towards these flexible, 'organismic' structures of school management.

Apart from Argyris and Schon's own experimental work, we cannot offer examples of training which meet the full criteria of team development. However we have had some contact with senior management teams in two Surrey schools who were attempting to review their working relationships. The following short account outlines the kinds of activities they engaged in.

The two schools were of comparable size and sharing similar philosophies. Each team was composed of the head, two deputies and a senior teacher. The objectives of their experiment were for each team to review and assess its own performance, to exchange experiences during the process of review and to engage subsequently in such further action as each might wish. There were three distinct phases:

Meetings in school

Over a period of three months, each team, in addition to normal meetings, held four special meetings devoted entirely to examining and assessing its performance and to investigating ways of improving its effectiveness. Consideration was given to the team's policy-making function, its composition and organisation, the conduct of team meetings and the nature of internal communications.

One of the heads on the project team attended all these meetings and agreed to produce background papers on issues raised by the teams, including self analysis by team members, the nature of teams, organisational structures and management styles.

A record was kept of each meeting and exchanged between teams, as were copies of all internal papers (job specifications, policy documents, etc.) tabled during meetings.

Out of school exercise

The two teams met for a weekend to exchange ideas and experiences. Each team prepared a question and a presentation for the other.

Questions:

from school X: What strategies were employed in order to develop a policy for the new management team from the presumably different styles of the two merging schools?

from school Y: Would you, on the whole, advocate that senior management teams should retain certain roles which probably reflect their interest and expertise, or do you think they and the school would gain from changing tasks?

Presentations:

by school X: 'Towards participation in management': an argument for blurring specialist roles within the senior team.

by school Y: 'Changing the school day': a case study illustrating the senior team's role in this innovation.

The teams also requested some specialist inputs on recent work on team management and team building. Two sessions were devoted to this.

In the final session the teams considered possible future action. They decided to meet together again after separate reflection on the experience.

Further work

Five weeks after the weekend meeting, the two teams met again. It was decided to continue the exploration of the different emphasis between the teams on the rotation of roles and responsibilities. This led to a more careful analysis of the way each team dealt with particular issues, and thence to an exploration of their various perspectives of the 'senior team': its identity, membership and purpose. Unfortunately, the pressures of industrial action limited the progress of the review at this stage. However the teams intended later to continue with the work.

The Dimension of Development External to the School

The concept of teamwork in educational management and the need for flexible, 'organismic' structures of management extends beyond the school to include work between heads, officers and inspectors. Many of the changes in educational policies and programmes currently being pressed upon schools can only be achieved by co-ordinated local activity.

We offer one example of a training experience designed to support and promote this kind of local collaboration. It is currently being developed by the London Borough of Merton with the Sussex Regional School Management Programme. As with several of the examples offered, it is at the time of writing in an early stage of development and no conclusive results have emerged. However, the following description outlines the broad structure and intentions, and serves to indicate the area where further experimentation may be of value.

The purpose of the course was described by the Authority thus:

> Education generally, and especially secondary schools, face new challenges in the next few years. The autonomy of heads and the separate specialisms of inspectors are a potential handicap in developing strategies for the implementation of LEA policies and Government intiatives. Clearly, neither group can ignore what is happening and it is vital that all learn to work together so that, through corporate action:
>
> *Specific issues* are taken up properly and professionally; and,
>
> *Policies and plans* are implemented as effectively and efficiently as possible.
>
> Hence a major objective of the course must be to improve and develop the skills of working together on issues of common concern. The course will provide opportunities for the ten secondary heads and six inspectors to work together on joint tasks of educational planning, development and evaluation. It will encourage them to reflect on this experience and to formulate plans for further joint action after the course ends.

Participants will be expected to have regular contact during the course with the Deputy Director of Education who will direct the exercise and be fully involved in the discussion of future action.

A twenty-four day course has been planned to span the school year 1985/6. The course falls into three units:

Introduction to joint action
This consists of a one day meeting to discuss the broad purpose of the course followed by a five day residential session offering close support for the group's first attempts to work together. This workshop is organised with the help of an industrial management trainer and introduces the heads and inspectors to the ICI approach to the management of change in organisations.

Policy development and evaluation
Eleven days are devoted to an investigation of current practice in Merton at school and LEA level.

Three single days are allocated to the following tasks:
- a close analysis of various Merton documents relating to policy development and evaluation;
- an empirical examination of curriculum planning and evaluation in their own school (for the heads), and of the involvement of inspectors at LEA and school levels (for the inspectors).

At the second residential session, the group completes this analysis of current practice, comparing it with practice elsewhere. Then, working in small task groups, the heads and inspectors consider areas for improvement and formulate plans for development work over the next few months. Five more days of release are allocated in support of this work. Each group has the services of an experienced head from another authority who provides 'secretariat' support. The groups report progress to the Deputy Director of Education who chairs all plenary sessions and is responsible for the overview of developments and their implications for future policy and practice in Merton.

Staff development for school and authority
In the third residential session and the remaining single days, a second cycle of review and development is begun with a similar

pattern of work.
Further action.
There is a final plenary session to consider the opportunities for further joint action. Beyond this, inspectors will be encouraged to consider the implications of the experience for their understanding of their own roles within the authority. Heads too will need to examine the consequences for their internal management organisation.

In this example, the authority has seen the opportunity, through the national initiative, to bring together a key group of people – the inspectors and secondary heads – to re-examine the way they might work together in response to the challenges which currently face the education service. In addition to this, they will also attempt a re-assessment of two important areas of the education service: policy development and implementation, and staff-development. Given the timescale of the exercise, they can only expect limited success. But even so, this could be a major gain to the authority in terms of its future operations.

References

ARGYRIS, C and SCHON, D 1974 *Theory in practice: increasing professional effectiveness* London: Jossey Bass

ARGYRIS, C and SCHON, D 1978 *Organisational learning: a theory of action perspective* Reading, Mass: Addison Wesley

BUCKLEY, J 1985 'How training needs are being met: Sweden' in *The training of secondary school heads in Western Europe* Windsor: NFER/Nelson

BURNS, T 1963 'Industry in a new age' *New Society* No.18 31.1.63

GREAT BRITAIN: DEPARTMENT OF EDUCATION AND SCIENCE 1983 *The in-service teacher training grants scheme Circular 3/83* London: DES

HUGHES, M CARTER, J and FIDLER, B 1981 *Professional development provision for senior staff in schools and colleges* University of Birmingham, Department of Social and Administrative Studies in Education

KOLB, D and FRY, R 1975 'Towards an applied theory of experiential learning' in C Cooper (ed) 1975 *Theories of group processes* London: Wiley

RICHARDSON, J and BENNETT, B 1984 'Applying learning techniques to on-the-job development' *Journal of European Industrial Training* Vol 8 Nos 1, 3 and 4 pp3-7, 5-10 and 3-7 respectively

CHAPTER SIX

Comments and Observations from the Field

This chapter draws on field reports to present the direct experience of headteachers and others in their attempts to improve their management capabilities. The extracts are selected to illuminate some of the key activities described in earlier chapters.

Comments on the Use of Self-Development Activities

In Chapter Three we described the self-development workshops which were designed and organised by the project. The three reports summarised below were submitted by two headteachers and an educational administrator who took part in the experimental workshop.

Self Development Exercises: a Short Experiment

As a four week exercise I find it difficult to assess any level of success in my attempts at self-development exercises. As a move in a specific direction I found it interesting. A brief background would help to set the scene. Apart from the strictures of industrial action, we also have two major developments occurring within the school:

> a complete revamp of our lower school curriculum;
>
> the establishment of our full school Review, alongside the formation of our school and departmental two-year strategy.

I mention these areas because of their time-consuming nature. Consequently, I found it difficult to involve many others in this trialling exercise, but instead looked initially at exercises I could operate alone.

The working day: keeping a diary (two weeks)

I found the idea of regular time slots difficult to fill. I knew that breaking down activities into ten minute units would be a non-starter so I attempted half-hour segments. After two days I reverted to a format suggested by a previous exercise of merely noting start and finish times of each activity. The actual recording did not prove to be as arduous as I expected and I rarely found myself with chunks of time for which I could not account.

Analysis of material proved rather disconcerting. I set aside time (usually fifteen minutes) at the end of each day to review the range of activities and found it akin to costing a budget account – when I last attempted that activity I found I was spending considerably more than I earned! The use of the critical incident approach was useful and here I did find an area for potential saving. I had always decried the growth of the notion of headship yet when I reviewed the various crises I found a disproportionate use of senior management time – I simply would not let go, despite the fact that I have two excellent deputies. We talked about this at some length and I have now adopted a more prudent approach. Similarly, I have found that an organisational weakness thrown up by the diary centres on the heads of department. Having spoken to them we are setting up an INSET day next term on the role of the HOD.

Meetings review (three weeks)

The current dispute has, to some extent, prevented a great deal of work in this area, but two specific cases did allow some investigation.

> The curriculum group (an open meeting) has been engaged in a review of the foundation year's programme. Their brief, under the chairmanship of a deputy, was to start from scratch and design an ideal world from which we could move. This included the flying of a number of philosophical kites. To say the meetings were loose was to understate. This structure, while democratically useful, was almost its own downfall. I asked two of the team to acquaint themselves with the approaches covered by the meetings questionnaire, and then to record their own feelings after each meeting. After three such meetings (they were meeting two or three times a week) I met them with the chairman and we analysed their findings.

Despite their desire for democracy, they desperately sought greater structure or leadership and we therefore discussed the role of the chairman. The exercise continued over the next two meetings with results: the rate of progress increased; the feeling of achievement increased; the 'democratic nature' remained the same.

> We have recently set up a joint Governor/Staff Working Party to co-ordinate our School Review. These meetings are far

more formal and as yet have not actually set about the potentially difficult task of conducting the Review. I asked the chairman of this group (Vice-Chairman of Governors) to join me in completing the questionnaire for the two meetings held within the three week trial period. They did not really throw up anything that was not already predictable.

Working on Self-development with Other Members of the Senior Team

My two deputies gave me invaluable help in assessing the work of the materials we tested together, and the fact that we were able to be completely frank and open about what we discovered about ourselves and each other in the process made the task meaningful and worthwhile. I am not exaggerating when I say that it strengthened our relationship considerably.

Coping with stress

The first thing we did was to name the sources of stress which we experienced at various times: colleagues; pupils; parents; neighbours of the school; unions; governors; the LEA; HMI; the media; family; friends; ourselves.

We then carried out the appropriate self-development exercise, and referred back to the suggested ways in which people reduce stress to see if we could identify any of the proposed methods in our own coping behaviour. We found that we frequently avoided difficult issues initially, before carrying out a protracted filtering out of the important factors until we reached the point where most personal uncertainty was largely eradicated, although not entirely. We then tended to share the problem with other people, not so as to create more guilt, but to find an agreed way forward. Uncertainty shared is anxiety weakened. Autocracies encourage certainty, whereas democracies promote learning.

Finally, we also agreed that experience teaches us that the stressful situation we fear is never in practice as bad as it seems at first sight. Stress can be exhilarating as well as debilitating. Just talking about it with other people is therapeutic.

Critical blockages survey

We did this test separately and then came together to discuss the results.

We found it comforting to have strengths as well as weaknesses, although it took us some time to accept the information revealed by the scores. It made us go back to the individual questions to find out if we had been guilty of self-deception, and when it became evident that we had not, we began to come to terms with a view of ourselves which we had not previously admitted to seeing. Self-exposure can be a painful business.

However, it was encouraging to find that our combined strengths more than compensated for our individual weaknesses. This I think, is the strength of a team approach as long as the members of the team are prepared to be honest with each other.

The discovery of a weakness creates the need for appropriate training to remedy the problem.

Organisation behaviour describer survey

We did this as a combined exercise which centred upon a senior member of the teaching staff. We agreed which box to tick, usually unhesitatingly, and occasionally after some discussion.

We found it most interesting to concentrate our attention upon the perceived behaviour of a colleague. The strengths and weaknesses revealed indicated the need for in-service training of a kind which would limit emotional expressiveness and intensify consideration. Here was a classic example of a person with drive, initiative and imagination shackled by a personality which aroused antagonism and took too little account of other people's ideas and feelings. Our fear was that no amount of training would bring about the required change in behaviour because it was too fundamental and deep-rooted to be altered significantly. How, in fact, do you confront someone with such a destructive analysis of his professional conduct and persuade him to accept the criticism and to strive to change his style of working? And yet, surely the whole point of identifying undesirable behaviour is to improve it for the benefit of all involved in the work situation. This is one of the dilemmas posed by staff appraisal.

The OBD Survey, we feel, could be a very useful tool in the writing of references. It helps to pinpoint many important factors which are essential in the creation of an accurate pen portrait of the person under scrutiny.

Interpreting yourself and others

We approached the exercise with some anxiety at first because, although we deliberately chose five other people as guinea-pigs, we knew we had to place ourselves on the scale linking their opposing characteristics to complete the study. What helped us to face up to this potentially threatening situation was the fact that we had been working together for the past eleven years and we are good friends as well as colleagues. We worked out the different dimensions together and then placed ourselves without consultation on the scale for each of the ten dimensions. We then exchanged papers and left the cross where it was if we agreed with its position, or put the cross in a different place if we disagreed. Finally, we gave our reasons for any changes we had made.

In my opinion the value of this kind of work is considerably increased if it can be undertaken as a co-operative venture. There is a real danger that one's own perception of oneself is faulty in certain respects, and it is enlightening and helpful to have a trusted colleague who is willing to give an honest appraisal and back it up with telling evidence. It certainly discourages you from coming to hasty conclusions about other people, and provides an opportunity to go into their strengths and weaknesses in some detail. Again, there are obvious implications for in-service training and staff development, including the possibility of job exchanges.

Perceptions of your organisation

Again we found it extremely valuable to complete a checklist separately before discussing our conclusions in detail. This helped us to clarify strengths and reveal weaknesses.

We agreed that our departmental structure is the source of competition and insularity on occasions which often hinders co-operation and breeds mistrust, if not downright jealousy. The need for staff to accept and understand a whole school policy designed to work for the good of all the pupils was recognised, rather than to engage in activities designed to promote one-upmanship which can be a disintegrating practice. The question remains: how can we persuade people who prefer tunnel vision to take a broader view of the educational process without doing serious damage to their self-esteem?

Increasingly it seems clear that it would be beneficial for all teaching staff to be exposed to the agony and the ecstasy involved in working through this kind of exercise because it is very revealing. Generally accepted conclusions may well lead to helpful change.

Meetings review

We thought this review called into question traditional practice within the school and made us think very carefully about the eight criteria against which the selected meeting would be measured. The usefulness of this procedure lies in the fact that it provides a ready-made tool for evaluation which would be energy-sapping and time-consuming to compile oneself. An uneasy feeling that all is not right with meetings can be so easily transformed into the pleasing certainty that we can identify what is wrong and try to correct it.

We looked at main staff meetings and came to the conclusion that openness and energy were noticeable by their absence because of the size of the group. To improve the effectiveness of the proceedings we have decided to issue detailed information in advance of the meeting, thus limiting the need for interminable discussion caused by lack of knowledge. Working Party reports and recommendations will be presented similarly for rubber-stamping, particularly if the groundwork has been done properly.

Conclusions

It has been an extremely valuable experience to make time in order to look calmly and objectively at techniques and processes which assist management self-development. For too much of our working lives we are dealing with routine matters and reacting to events as they occur, with little opportunity for reflection and self-examination.

It definitely helps to share the soul-searching with trusted colleagues who can be relied upon to remove any traces of self-delusion.

It would be very useful to have access to a wide range of materials of this kind which have particular relevance to education so that they could be used appropriately as necessary.

A Personal View of Self-Development by an Educational Administrator

From a continuing process of self-questioning and the experience of the workshop I have drawn up a personal agenda for self-development. I regard this as a first stage, but also an aspect of all stages since reflection is part of my life and self-development represents to me a continuing dialogue of career evaluation and experimentation. I have focussed on a few key areas where I identify a need for development. I hope to use a selection of materials and literature noted during this workshop as an aid to clarifying and locating more specifically areas for development.

Acceptance and valuation of myself

I see a need to acknowledge and own my personal priorities and judgements. To do this I need to say no to some demands made on me and state assertively my priorities. In saying no I need to practise ensuring that I take responsibility for my decision, avoid rejection of 'askers' as people and leave them in a position to evaluate their consequent actions openly.

I also need to learn to recognise that some tasks and some relationships are 'wild cards' with which it is pointless to engage beyond a certain point. I find this problematic and think the relation of this to the need to learn and to guard against increasing rejection and avoidance needs vigilance.

I also need to value and own the good things I have achieved. I need unaggressively to help others to do this, abandoning the "Well I know I've done a good job and that's all that matters" reaction – since that involves 'flight' and a sense of inner separateness and 'superiority'. I need to learn to take and receive openly. I need to accept myself as someone who cannot always be giving and who has needs. This workshop is a form of taking which I value – I must eschew all temptation to imply I was doing it 'for the authority...', etc. – or to 'justify' it.

Finally, I must continue to accommodate my decision/ attempts to retain my female positive strengths within my management style whilst working through and/or, if necessary, accepting more negative aspects of behaviour based on stereotypes. This means positively relating to women and men managers as people but scrutinising sex stereotyped underlying behaviours in myself and others.

I need to create and maintain personal space for health, career, study, etc.

Learning to value and relate to organisations

Organisations, like individuals, have careers and histories. I need to explore my frustrations with some of the manifestations of this such as resistance to change, defence of empires, in terms of developing and understanding the 'whole' organisation in the same way as I am developing understandings of individuals as whole people rather than role fillers.

Developing my personal presentation

I want to explore and develop strategies for dealing with naked aggression. I want to explore and develop strategies for maintaining other people's perceptions of perceived changes in myself in order to prevent 'overkill" and to interact sensitively.

Strategies for development

I have identified several strategies for developing in different areas.

- A Journal: I hope to complete a weekly journal in which I will review the last week and identify potential critical points in the coming week. I hope to use the three main headings and the sub-themes in my evaluation to shape the journal.
- Individual dialogue with an individual: I hope to develop my understanding of self-development as a whole (conceptually and in practice) with my partner. I hope to develop sensitivity to the organisation and positive values for myself through this medium.
- Dialogue with subordinates: I hope to develop sensitivity to the milieu, notions of myself as a receiver (? and as a positive creator). These will, I hope, be areas for development with my staff as a shared learning experience.
- Dialogue with my boss: I sense an interest but also a true problem in self-development with my 'boss' – insofar as one exists. I think I could learn a lot about acknowledging personal priorities and achievement and acceptance of wild cards in this way. I shall try to engage with him in whatever areas he shows a response to.

Practical tasks: an aide memoire

- Work through materials. Establish whether any require very detailed examination.
- Start journal.
- Establish communication/contract with partner: follow up pre-workshop discussion on what is self-development. Work through evaluation and identify any areas where specific contracts might be negotiable.
- Work through evaluation and relevant material (summary) with boss. Explore the possibility of establishing a contract – focus this [because of] time pressure. Express my need for this explicitly.
- At next section meeting, explore the possibility of a joint learning experience – my self development – their self or task related development. Identify areas of work and training materials relevant to this.
- Scan Education/TES/THES to try to develop thoughts on

personal career development as an adjunct to evaluation area.
- Feedback from workshop into network and explore its value and materials.

The Same Administrator's Report to the Society of Education Officers

I was asked to participate in a short residential course and follow-up programme on self-development for managers through Sussex University. The self development course was prepared jointly by SEO, University of Sussex and the Local Government Training Board. Once nominated I was also contacted by SEO.

The course was identified for me as a pilot project in explaining the use of self-development for Education Officers using course members and collected written materials as a springboard, and using a programme of personal self-development as both an end in itself and an evaluation of the project. There was some confusion amongst course members about the commitment to undertaking a personal programme and this generated some tension and disagreement within the residential workshop. This was resolved by members splitting into groups or individuals whose self-allotted tasks varied from designing a training programme for others, on the basis of identifying roles and tasks, to developing a 'contract' for self-development using the materials and course members. Some of the confusion seemed to arise from different expectations in discussions with nominators and some from the inherent difficulty of tackling self-development. In my view, which has strengthened as I have followed through the project, this points to the importance of preparation before joining courses which are based on notions of individual responsibility for learning and which address issues of self-awareness rather than skills and tasks. For a nationally-based course the logistical problems in pre-course preparation through personal contact are overwhelming but this might be possible on a regional basis.

All aspects of the course, properly in my view, concentrated on the responsibility of individuals for developing their own agenda and for contributing fully to the shape of the course. However, this creates a difficult role for facilitators, who sometimes translate this as a need to be totally passive. The balance is very difficult, but for officers meeting from wide backgrounds, used to role-based bureaucracies, it is important for such courses to provide structured, secure opportunities for self reflection. This was exemplified well at the one-day follow-up session some three months later where, in the morning, time was used in a structured way to give each individual his own 'space' to describe the implementation of his contract. In the afternoon a free agenda dissolved somewhat into a talking session for more voluble course members. I do not see any problem in facilitators structuring time, in agreement with members, when the content of discussion is as high risk as probing deeply personal effectiveness.

The course team had collected a compendious library of self development materials, some of which were excellent, some dangerously mechanistic. Along with several other course members, I selected a range of materials for self evaluation purposes and working this through with others, developed a framework of self evaluation. This in itself involved developing a much clearer notion of the importance and relevance of self-evaluation for work. Roughly we agreed that self analysis might equate to a statement of the current state of play of an individual in terms of strengths, weaknesses, etc. Self evaluation would relate the understanding of strengths and weaknesses to personal value systems and choices and the value systems and choices of the organisation. Self-development would be a process of exploring tensions between organisational and personal perspectives and identifying areas and tasks where development is most important to the individual and then using the materials and other activities to develop.

On the basis of the initial evaluation, I selected further materials, almost exclusively from a Manpower Services Commission manual, which proved to be very probing and unmechanistic. In the period since the initial workshop, I have worked through a substantial number of these. From these exercises I have developed clearer insights into sources of stress and issues where I have not previously been satisfied with my performance. I have then used a weekly journal to examine the previous week against the issues identified and explore successes and failures. Following from this I have also used the journal to review the coming week to identify potential points of difficulty and consider likely strategies in the light of my self evaluation and previous activities as set out in the journal. A salutory, difficult, positive, time-consuming exercise! In addition I have discussed the exercise and some of my personal perspectives with two colleagues, both of whom have also worked through some of the exercises and started to address their own issues of self development. I have also 'shared' this exercise with the Head of my Authority's Training Centre who is interested in this form of training which relates closely to the Authority's experience of racism awareness and sexism awareness training.

At the follow-up one day meeting with course members each member described his or her own processes of implementation which varied enormously. About 50% of course members attended and a further 15% were keen, but unable to do so. One other member had chosen a reflection process to support self development and had found this enormously useful. Others had chosen to involve colleagues in developing local programmes for self development and support. Others still had used specific projects as a focus for their self-development. The list below describes the consensus of key issues which had arisen:

- the problem of finding time and organisational acceptance for self development. Actors in the education service focus hard on serving and responding to officers and it is difficult to maintain a sense of the importance of self-development as an integral part of improving management effectiveness;
- is there such a thing as management self development? The managerial process is so integrative that the process must be seen in relation to others and the organisation;
- it is almost impossible to do it totally alone. The process needs to be shared for support, motivation and feedback;
- there are different states of readiness and personal style which make different approaches important. Self development cannot effectively be imposed and its implementation must be appropriate to the individual;
- the interaction between pain and growth within self-learning;
- the shape of different relevant support processes, e.g. books, journals, reflection, discussion, networks of individuals, etc.;
- the importance of developing a managerial environment which fosters self-development and institutionalised change;
- the importance of taking responsibility for your own development;
- the difficulties for teachers in developing a changing perspective of their roles as managers, teachers and learners;
- a consciousness of the different management roles of individuals.

For the future I will try to continue the programme as described. Motivation is difficult for all involved with self-development but even small successes help. I am also involved in discussions with LGTB and the Authority's Training Centre on pursuing this kind of programme. Some course members are working on an input on self-development for managers for the summer conference, drawing on the materials and on the pilot experience. For some managers this seems to be a very important form of training, but its appropriateness depends heavily upon the readiness and motivation of the individual and the available support.

One final point of interest. One participant/consultant to the course was a man nominated by the Confederation of British Industry who, from a point of some apparent initial ambivalence, proved to be a very useful focus in dealing with several key issues and an important colleague as a 'neutral' outside observer.

Experiences of Keeping a Journal

Keeping a journal is one of the strategies for personal development discussed in Chapter Three. Some of those involved in testing out new ideas in the context of the project agreed not only to keep a journal over a substantial period of time, but also to evaluate some of its implications.

The two examples given here offer a number of contrasts. The first is a report of an interview conducted by a member of the project team; the second an autobiographical comment. The first journal-keeper is a head; the second an educational administrator. The first journal was undertaken on request; the second was an entirely voluntary activity. Despite these differences, the extracts show some important similarities, especially in their comments on the therapeutic aspects of journal writing and the value of the resulting journal as a tool for professional reflection.

Responding to the Day's Events

This extract is drawn from an extensive interview with a recently appointed headteacher who has just completed a twenty day basic course in school management.

During the course, which Miss M found in general very useful, "particularly the chance to talk through real issues and real problems with other heads", she was asked by the course director if she would like to start keeping a journal (of her work in school – not of the course). Two other recently appointed heads were asked to do the same. She agreed "because I thought it would be used as a basis for discussion between [the director] and the three of us". Miss M testified several times to the fact that she sees "talking things through" with other heads and with others interested/experienced in schools as a very useful and powerful tool in her own personal development. The journal begins on 19th January, 1984, and the last entry is dated 11th April, 1984. It takes the form of a personal response by Miss M to the day's events in her school. This is what she says she was asked to do, "He didn't want just a diary of events. It was meant to be more emotional, thoughtful".

Looking back on the experience, Miss M. was unsure about the practical managerial value of the journal. "Writing it down probably did help clarify things for me but it didn't lead to me taking any action". In fact the journal is full of examples of Miss M taking action, particularly in the arena of staff relationships (e.g. difficulties with one of her deputies, dealing with a teacher whose dress offended her) but also with regard to option systems and relations with feeder primary schools. Whether these actions were indirectly engendered as a result of writing the journal is impossible to prove, but there is a sense of cataclysm about the 'before' and 'after' entries which suggest that the act of writing the journal helped towards action.

It is clear that Miss M saw the journal as being written if not entirely for someone else, at least, at someone else's behest and possibly for their benefit too:

> "I suppose I don't regret doing it because it hasn't done me any harm. I feel slight resentment because of the time it took. I feel slightly peeved because I put a lot of effort into it for someone else".

It is clear too that Miss M saw the original suggestion as leading to much more shared discussion than it did:

> "I stopped doing it when I saw it wasn't being used as I thought it would be... After I'd stopped I felt too peeved to want to take it up again".

Reading the journal and talking to this head reveal that she gained a great deal from keeping the journal. As a piece of reflective professional writing it is clear that she required more by way of support than the journal alone could provide. Indeed, at least to counterbalance the time and effort needed to complete the journal, she needed support, in the form of regular peer group discussions, in order to continue with the journal itself, "I'm not a great reader. I certainly wouldn't want more self-help package things. I'm much more of a doer and a talker and a learner by experience". Yet clearly she has 'done' much more than she would say she has. Reflective journal writing would therefore appear to be a good way into regular professional development for a head, but it requires the psychological support for some of regular 'use' of the journal in conjunction with peer group discussion.

Sources of support revealed by the journal are manifold. I have listed below those to whom Miss M either turned for help in moments of need or gained support from in their general interest in her and the school:

- Her deputies: Despite very real personality clashes she clearly sought and in the end obtained support from this source.
- The Chairman of governors: The most regularly mentioned source of support, both in general terms and over a specific issue (the replacement of a secretary).
- Other participants on the twenty day course.
- A secondary adviser.
- Previous colleagues, including those met on earlier courses: "I ring them two or three times a term for a chat and have rung them for specific help and advice".
- Colleague heads in the LEA: especially those most local and in similar size schools.
- The Director of Education: a pre-arranged "how are you settling in?" visit.
- 'AC', whose job role is not clear from the journal but who clearly provides both professional support, another woman's view, and personal support.
- The Education Welfare Officer for the school.
- The Area Education Officer.
- A local representative of her national association (SHA).

Despite the above evidence some journal entries reveal occasions when this head felt a need for support which was not immediately available:

1st February:	"I feel desperately depressed and in need of someone to talk to so I'll talk to my journal".
29th March:	"I wish I knew who I could consult to ask how to cope with very rude X".
2nd April:	"I keep on saying it but I do not know how to

> handle this and do not know who to turn to, to advise and help me".

Both the latter comments were written when Miss M felt very isolated within the school and experienced little or no support from her immediate colleagues.

Keeping and Using a Journal

I try to complete a longish entry on a Sunday, using my working diary as an aide memoire. I keep a fairly large working diary about me all the time and use coloured page liners to make 'do' lists and to note particular points of interest or comments. I use this diary to complete the journal because seeing a diary entry triggers a memory that is fairly complete and only overlaid by subsequent events in a general sense. Somehow, looking at a one line entry which earlier in the week *directed* me to the next meeting, releases memory more fully. In any case, without a structure, I personally would forget important things, or things which subsequently turn out to be important.

During 1985 I have also used the journal as an aide to a fairly specific programme of self-development. At the outset I undertook a 'contract' wherein I identified several key areas of stress or potential difficulty. Under four or five major headings I worked through some self analysis material to get greater clarity about specific areas for development. I then, when reviewing each week, included a review of how I had reacted to any circumstances covered by the headings, considered why I had reacted as I had and where appropriate in what ways I would prefer to act. I then reviewed the coming week under the same headings and explored in the journal any likely points where issues for development might arise. As this process built up, week by week I used the journal, through re-reading it – often quite a surprise – to build up strategies and to affirm progress and to try to understand and accept lack of it. This is a time-consuming discipline and requires some strength if you're feeling down. I usually end up feeling supported through a sense of purpose but during writing there is some pain in acknowledging failure or simply reliving disasters not of your making.

A final point about the journal for me is one of style. At first it's easy to feel self-conscious but a formal report style shapes comments and memories and takes on a life of its own. In the end I think I write as I would converse with a friend or fairly close colleague. This includes some personal comments and expression and exploration of feelings. I don't find this self-indulgent, though I feared I might, because by doing it regularly over a fairly extended period and by including some self-analysis, the processes of reading and writing interact.

Generally, although not easy, I find the process of journal entry very useful at the time, and sometimes quite a relief. I certainly find the process of reading and re-reading useful. For research purposes I have also found the journal to provide a wealth of clarity about events and interconnections, a depth of focus about my own and other people's value judgements and one route through complex events which is not one-dimensional and which conveys the pluralistic nature of the policy process in which I am engaged.

Reports on Action Learning Experiments

We regard action learning as a potentially important component in management training and Chapter four provides a detailed description of the action learning set. Here we focus on attempts to integrate action learning within the course. In 1983/4, two training programmes for secondary heads deliberately introduced action learning into the course itself in an attempt to extend the influence of training on managerial action in schools. Reports by the two teams responsible for these experiments, at the University of Bristol and Sussex, are offered here.

The View from Bristol

''Action learning' as a method has many interpretations, but we believe the one we used is close to that intended by Professor Reg Revans of Manchester Institute of Technology, its originator. We divided the eighteen members into three groups of six, mixed by LEA, type of experience, length of service and role as head or officer/adviser. Each group member had thirty minutes per unit to present a problem on which he was working in his school or office to the other five members of his/her group, to seek help from them in clarifying the problem and generating a variety of solutions. The decision about what to do remained the sole responsibility of the individual, who would report back at the next unit on the progress achieved to date and the problems encountered. This would lead to further problem analysis and the search for alternative solutions.

The group was given a highly structured procedural model to organise their thinking and presentation in the early stages, although it was made clear from the start that the group was self-regulating and retained the autonomy to decide its own work pattern and methods should the model prove inappropriate. Each group was, however, strongly advised to abide by the approach whereby the individual made an uninterrupted presentation for 10-15 minutes, followed by discussion concentrating on his problem alone, avoiding all anecdotal contributions from others about what they had done or might do in similar circumstances. It is crucial if any depth of analysis is to be reached and real trust built up that the presenter remains the only focus of attention during his period of presentation. The two directors and the evaluator decided not to take on the set adviser role, but moved round the groups in turn. This was partly due to lack of confidence in taking on the role, and partly from the desire to know what was going on in each group...

By unit three the groups had become established, the initial stages of problem analysis had been completed and people were beginning to work on the solution in their organisations. Comments at this stage fell into two categories: those relating to the task of action learning and those relating to the operation of the group. The latter were far more numerous than the former in March.

Groups emphasised the development of loyalty, trust and cohesion within the groups. Most members experienced the groups as very supportive, so that the level of self-confidence was being built up. One member found the experience pleasant rather than demanding; one was not enjoying it at all. Other features noted were that the spread of group membership was breaking down LEA centred loyalty, although the geographical distribution of members was proving difficult where visits were being planned to coordinate with the action learning set problems. One group wondered if sufficient thought had been given to this aspect when drawing up groups.

As far as the task of operating through an action learning problem-solving methodology was concerned, some members were stil having difficulty in selecting an appropriate problem for discussion. The advisers and officers were meeting some barriers in trying to help heads develop a usefully deep perception of an LEA role. Nevertheless the interaction of heads and LEA staff was seen to be a vital part of the partnership the programme was intended to foster. Perhaps this difficulty in perception helped what the groups noted as the development of a valuable skill, that of constructive challenge to the assumptions on which individuals based their solutions. One group mentioned the value of the rich variety of solutions that were being created. At this stage there was enthusiastic, though minority, support for the view that action learning groups were the most valuable part of the programme.

The design team very largely shared the perceptions of the participants about how the three groups were operating and about the value of what was occurring within them. However, they noted that although the three groups, as expected, had developed different characteristics, one group was already, from their point of view, having problems. They did not stick to the advice about timing, method of presentation and the role of the others not presenting. Consequently, though the group appeared to enjoy each other's company, there was little challenging of assumptions or generation of alternative solutions.

By units five and six, the groups had experienced the full force of the methodology and were in a position to make much more detailed evaluations. The questions, both for discussion and individual written response, were now task-confined. There were two tasks to consider. How well were groups coping with the action learning methodology? How effective were the solutions individuals were working through in their own schools and offices? Answers now revealed much greater divergences, and the energy and commitment within the three groups was now consistently different. In summarising the results, individual responses may be exaggerated, since I am emphasising the extremes recorded. The impact, or lack of impact, on the job had become the dominant way of estimating the success of the method. Many individuals noted that they had succeeded in solving at least one problem. They attributed their success either to the different perspectives of, or range of solutions generated by, the group, or to greater self-confidence resulting from the mutual support within the group. The clarification of the problem resulting from questions from the group was seen as the basis for success. In contrast, two individuals felt they had had no success at all, and for another two, industrial action had halted the consultative meetings they needed to pursue their solution. A few members were still not sure how well they were doing, despite assurances from the group.

Two major problems impeded the effectiveness of the method, as the participants saw it. The first, the effects of industrial action, has already been mentioned, and that had other impacts, as well as modifying the proposed courses of action mentioned above, on the morale and commitment to staff involved in change. The other problem had already surfaced by unit three, that of selecting a problem of appropriate length and complexity for the time-scale available. Two members were still struggling with this in June. Another felt that his group was not sufficiently committed to sharing, and the allocation of presentation time was not being fairly handled. Officers were still finding some barriers in using heads constructively, although visits to LEA offices in June and July overcame some of the difficulties. One head was also finding problems in matching actions to the expectation of staff and parents.

Nevertheless, there was considerable support shown for action learning as a successful method of problem solving on the job. Evidence was based on the experiences mentioned above. Conditions for using the method successfully were seen to be the careful structuring of the group; thoughtful planning of presentations; the choice of a problem appropriate to the method, that is a medium term problem of some complexity, but not involving the whole staff at any depth of consultation! The strengths were widely seen as good clarification of issues and alternative lines of action, and the supportive interest of the group. A few members remained unconvinced about the method right to the end, and a few others felt it was less effective in July than it had been initially.

When asked to assess the effectiveness of their own group, as opposed to the methodology, the divergences were less individual than group based. Of the two groups which had made a good start, one was more convinced than ever that they were achieving success. They commended each other for providing challenge, clarification, support: a variety of views, summarised in the opinion that action learning groups were the best feature of the programme. Another group had developed some divergent views, though the majority were still very positive, while acknowledging that not everyone's experience was the same. They felt there had been some slipping of rigour and momentum. The third group remained cheerful on the whole, but were not giving each other much task-centred support – "about 50% effective" summed up several views. What had been learnt by individuals in all three groups was that action learning groups support and enhance problem solving, but it is still the individual who has to take the action in his/her own patch, so there can be no shifting of responsibility for outcomes.

Looking to the future, and possibilities of continued progress in action learning, opinions were divided. Some people felt that the action learning sets as such had reached their peak, and might well decline if pursued further. Many saw them transmuting into group consultancies after the end of the programme. Others thought that on the basis of the relationships which had been established, a network of mutual support would enable new problems to be discussed, despite the geographical distances involved. A few people felt that the sets would need to be regrouped if they were to survive and some of the earlier discipline and rigour would need to be reintroduced. A few were still unconvinced that there was any useful future; it would need the selection of an appropriate problem, an unsolved difficulty, and confidence in the group.

The design team's worries about one of the three groups had continued through the summer as they noted the difficulty the group had in filling the time allocated fruitfully. A few opinions in the final review that the method had been unsuccessful came as no surprise therefore. What the design team had also observed was the growing skill and confidence in analysing problems, the enthusiasm and commitment generally shown, and the revelation and sharing of major difficulties and deep reactions. They therefore decided that the idea of building and supporting a network of consultancy beyond the end of the progamme would be a valuable continuation of the learning already gained.

A final evaluation questionnaire asked participants to comment on the working relationships which had been achieved within the sets. Fourteen of the eighteen commented that they had been of considerable depth, very supportive, very successful in enabling good problem analysis and overall that the relationships in the sets had proved a basis for effective learning. There were also comments about the successful mixing of personalities and backgrounds: one member wondered how far it had been possible for the design team to plan this.

When the whole group discussed the outcomes of the course with four Chief Education Officers, action learning clearly emerged as the major method of ensuring that there was transfer from the programme to the job, and that other members of staff, particularly the senior management team, had become involved in the learning from the programme through it. This conclusion was reached despite the practical difficulties mentioned earlier in handling the methodology fully and effectively.

On balance, the design team think they were right to move round the groups, rather than attach themselves as advisers permanently to one group. However, we recognise that the advantage was of keeping an overview of the process, probably resulting in less than maximum learning for at least one of the three groups. The loss of momentum and rigour later, and difficulty in selecting a problem earlier, might have been avoided if we had taken a more traditional set adviser role.

The View from Sussex

In designing the course we had seen action learning as a natural fourth module to the course. The others were all based on the study of three guiding questions of immediate concern to all secondary heads and deputies. In each case, the course members had been asked to address these questions via practical exercises based on their experience and actual field research in their own schools.

We intended the action learning phase to do two things. It was to enable members to bring forward real management problems from their own schools and work on these with the support of others in their action learning sets. In this way the unreal, although practical, exercises of the first three modules would be replaced by real, live, action in the schools. Secondly, we hoped that the open-ended nature of the action learning sets would facilitate the continuance of mutual support and learning activities between the members after the formal end of the twenty day course.

After reading all we could find on action learning, we decided to consult one of its current leading exponents, David Casey. It was his writing on the problems of transfer of learning from course to job that had first given action learning a high profile with the course design team (Casey, 1980). Two members of the course team met him in London and discussed our ideas with him. He was later commissioned to play two roles for us.

He agreed to join us in presenting the idea of action learning to the whole course membership on day one of the five allotted to this module. He also agreed to act as adviser to the group of six set advisers since we all knew that this was a role of crucial importance and wanted the benefit of his experience as we began to practise it.

The Launch

Day one of this module was designed in two halves. In the morning, following a brief introduction, there were two speakers. Each had already been a member of an action learning activity and spoke directly from his own experience of action learning. One was the managing director of a medium-sized company engaged in the metal finishing business. The other was a member of the course planning team who had, coincidentally, enrolled himself on a commercial action learning programme in the term before the course design team first met.

After lunch, David Casey introduced the key elements of action learning to the course membership by simulating the real action learning set situation within mini-groups (of three or four) inside the lecture room. His main thrust lay in stressing the need for open, direct and supportive use of the process of mutual questioning on which action learning is founded.

The full course membership had been divided in advance of day one into six sets of five or six members, each of which had been allocated a set adviser. Four of these advisers came from the course planning team of seven. The other two were recruited from the wider constituency of the School of Education – one faculty member and one past MA student who was a practising head in the region. This group of six had its first meeting with David Casey before the full course membership convened on day one. The six sets also had the briefest of meetings with their advisers during the same day to fix the date of their first full set meeting.

Some outcomes

The planned schedule for the four remaining days of the twenty day course allowed for three meetings of each set during the summer term 1984 and one in early September. In this way, we hoped to signal the potential open-endedness of this part of the course programme.

In the event, this planning was affected by the industrial action taken by teacher unions in that period. This is the record of set meetings which actually took place.

Three of the six sets completed their full schedule, although only one recorded 100% attendance from members on each occasion. Of the other two, one had a very short and badly attended meeting for its last session and had generally met with one less than its full complement of members. The last of the three met on every scheduled occasion but always without one member of the set, a deputy who could not leave his school at all during the teachers' action.

Two of the other three sets met on three occasions each, although one of them consistently had one less than its full complement and the other was always two short: 'one member never came and another tried but failed every time'.

The sixth set never met at all. The first two meetings were arranged but cancelled during the summer term and the efforts of the adviser to rearrange these in September were frustrated by a clear negative response from two members and no response at all from the other three. Despite this very disappointing response to action learning, it was clear that, where regular set meetings did take place, members found action learning both acceptable and useful. All the reports of completed set meetings talked of useful exchanges between members in which the presenter of the management issue or problem was helped to "put his problem in focus", "redefine her own sense of the difficulty" or even "completely revise his view of what the real problem was".

Examples of this process of reframing or redefining were widespread. One member had presented his initial issue as one of the distribution of senior staff responsibilities between two deputies. Questioning from other members of his set led him to examine and eventually to concentrate on revising his own relationship with the two deputies concerned, the ways in which he demonstrated this to the other staff and the individual problems of one of the two deputies who clearly did not enjoy the role he was now being asked to play.

Another described a complex situation which appeared to be an amalgam of a shortage of qualified specialists in an important subject area compounded by a weakness in existing staffing, an ineffective allocation of salary points and difficulties in allocating suitable teaching space. All this was inhibiting his efforts to introduce a new discipline into the common curriculum in year three: in other words, a typical problem of headship. Through their effort to understand this situation, set members brought the presenter to a total re-examination of the existing curriculum. Then, in his attempts to explain to the set the current allocation of lesson time, he provided his own insight into the next logical step to be taken in solving the problem. The effect of the set's questions had been to help him clarify and ultimately prioritise all the different factors in the situation.

A third member asked for help in the preparation of her response to the LEA on the reduction of responsibility points to match falling rolls. Once more, discussion within the set brought her to her own conclusion that no satisfactory solution was likely to emerge by simply tinkering with the existing system of distribution. As a result of the set's questioning and requests for more information, she produced a full breakdown of the existing distribution. This revealed all the historical and personal reasons for the creation of certain posts, as well as the more obvious structural ones. From this base, the head was able to begin to plan towards a situation in which her own aspirations for the structures and rewards, in a medium sized school, could more nearly match the LEA allocation of points. In the shorter term, she acquired some useful (because rational and clearly understood) arguments to deploy with her LEA for some concessions on the way to achieving the reduced total.

Some conclusions

It is impossible to use this experience to assess fully the value of action learning to school management training. However, the limited evidence is positive; the set meetings which did take place provided valuable learning opportunities and many members took away much of value to them. At the same time, the organisers are far from satisfied with the outcomes. Teacher action in the summer term 1984 clearly weakened the commitment of members to course attendance. In these circumstances heads felt their presence in school was indispensible, and were unwilling to leave their deputies to shoulder the full responsibility. Notwithstanding this factor, our own review of the action learning element in the programme revealed organisational defects which, with hindsight, must have reduced the appeal and effectiveness of sets.

The constitution of the six groups was arrived at as the result of a deliberate policy to mix members from as many different LEAs as possible, whilst avoiding any obvious personality clashes. In the event, this meant that many members had very difficult journeys to make in order to attend set meetings. Given other problems, this undoubtedly contributed to the poor attendance.

Despite this policy of mixing heads from different LEAs, the sets remained both entirely educational, in job character terms, and largely composed of people who had already met each other on the course. The purest form of action learning stresses the value of 'an intelligent interloper asking idiot questions, expertly' (Revans, 1971). This quality was denied us by the nature of our exercise and at least three of the set advisers considered this a significant limitation.

However, the biggest problems arose because of confusion amongst set advisers as to their role, and a more general confusion amongst members and set advisers concerning the precise nature of the function and process of the set. For example, to the adviser who had himself participated in an action learning set previously, the essential and distinguishing features of action learning were twofold: one was to focus attention on the problem of each presenter in turn through a mixture of "idiot questions asked expertly" and a total avoidance of anecdotal reflection; the other was a commitment at each meeting to take some form of action before the next. To another adviser an intention to act was sufficient, whilst to a third "the purpose of these sets was not to solve the problem but to examine a way of redefining the problem by persistent questioning". The set advisers' review meeting did not resolve this difference of view. The debate closed with a reaffirmation (from one of the original course planning team) that failure to grasp the nettle of 'real, live action' between meetings had led to some set members seeking to avoid taking action, preferring the time honoured education course method of 'further discussion' as the 'solution' to a problem.

Despite our attempts to anticipate this problem by using David Casey as a process consultant, we were inadequately prepared. Using him as we did, we expected too much and the wrong things from him. He, in turn, in his wish to help us, was trying to do a job, fulfil a role, which he normally would deny wherever possible. As he says (Casey 1983), the role of the set adviser cannot be sharply delineated, and so, by definition, cannot be taught either; it can only be learned by 'doing' aided by thoughtful personal reflection. To attempt to launch action learning on this scale with our level of experience was far too optimistic. The uncertainty and confusion surrounding the workings of the sets clearly contributed to the sharply varying reactions of the set members.

The final problem arose out of our attempt to introduce action learning as the fourth element in a modular course. This undoubtedly compounded the other difficulties we experienced. Even though the other three modules had been based on both the considered reflection of the course members' own experiences and on real work exercises carried out as a part of each module, they had also been stimulated by external inputs and subjected to intensive group debate in generalised terms. Action learning, as a method of management learning, has no place for 'expert inputs' and general debate should be replaced by intensive, specific discussion of issues requiring action. The expectations of most course members were, therefore, at odds with action learning from the outset.

Courses have a beginning and an end; they are terminal by nature. This in itself is part of the problem of the transfer of learning from course to work. The action learning set is intended to continue in being as long as it stimulates useful action. The five course days allocated to action learning were intended only to launch the process not to see it concluded. But, because these five days were perceived to be part of a course being held in the 1983/84 school year, the sets did not continue beyond that lifespan.

The main conclusion on this issue at the set advisers' final meeting was that action learning should not, indeed could not, be a fourth module of the course in future. It should be built in as a normal part of course methodology from the outset. This has been done for the 1985 Sussex course and, at the time of writing, seems to have led to a much greater degree of success in terms of the use of action learning than we experienced in 1984. Although the value of this form of action learning is testified to in reports on other courses in educational management (Ballinger, 1984), it is questionable whether this is in fact action learning at all as Revans or Casey et al would see it. That is *not* to recant on its value as a learning method to be employed on education management courses. Rather, it is to give it a better definition than action learning.

What the Sussex 1985 and other courses might perhaps be better described as doing is building into their structures a reliance on the personal responsibility of course members for their own 'learning through doing'; a form of learning plan more attributable to the work of Kolb, Rubin and McIntyre (Kolb et al, 1979) than to the contributions made by Revans.

It is even questionable whether action learning, as originally conceived, can ever be practised successfully as a *part* of a *course*. It is perhaps too much of a holistic concept in its own right. Any attempt to integrate it within a larger training experience with competing structures and pre-occupations will always create problems. A better approach may be to launch action learning as a support activity for corporate action after management training.

Support After School Management Training

We select two reports which focus on the question of how

management training courses can best be followed up and supported when the participants have returned to their own settings. The first item, based on interviews with heads who attended twenty day courses, suggests that a significant amount of continuing support tends to come from friendly colleagues, whether they were first met on the course or whether they were known professionally before that. The second extract is taken from a report concerning a generally successful thirty day course where, nonetheless, advisers and LEA officers remained largely uninvolved in preparations for the course or in the discussion of heads' subsequent needs.

An Analysis of Interviews with Heads

This field report offers an impressionistic account of ten interviews held with head teachers who have attended twenty day basic courses in school management. The interviews were not focussed specifically on follow up support, but they yielded many valuable insights.

The heads interviewed had acquired their skills and knowhow from a variety of origins. Most had been on courses of various kinds, ranging from one-week COSMOS courses run by HMI to one- or two-day courses put on by the Secondary Heads Association, and covering not only specialised topics such as timetabling but broad themes such as secondary education in the eighties. However, these forms of provision were on the whole considered to generate factual information rather than ideas, and limited technical abilities rather than broadly-applicable skills.

Many of the heads took the view that their own experience of varied aspects of school management had been the best preparation for their jobs. All had served as deputies, and the majority had previously been heads of department, pastoral heads, or both. Such experience had steadily built up their confidence in their management capabilities. But in addition, a particularly important source of learning had been the experience of working closely with other heads. Quite commonly, a single role model was identified ("I learned almost all I know about headship from Joe Smith"); but sometimes the indebtedness was to an amalgam of the admirable qualities of two or three key people. Nor were the prototypes always favourable; heads were able to learn how not to do the job from notably unsuccessful seniors, as well as being able to model themselves on good exemplars of the craft of headship.

It was interesting, in the light of such discussions, to learn how clearly LEAs themselves would appear to believe in the wisdom of experience. None of the heads, on taking up post, was offered any significant form of induction to his or her task, and one very recently-appointed head confessed to a sense of some confusion and disorientation as a result. At most, it appeared, a new head might be offered a day's tour round County Hall or a half day visit by the Divisional Education Officer.

Given, then, that the ten heads in question reckoned to have picked up most of their know-how so far by following others' examples and by learning on-the-job, what could one say of their future possible modes of knowledge acquisition and professional support? One point emerged quite clearly from the interviews, namely that heads do not find time for any extensive reading. Some explained this in terms of the incessant pressures of the job; others spoke of themselves as doers rather than cogitators. But whatever the cause, there seems very little mileage in any support system based on printed material.

Another commonly-expressed reservation concerned the role of advisers in any pattern of follow-up to training opportunities. The main problem here was seen to be the very heavy load which advisers already carry, at least in the authorities represented, and their consequent lack of availability. The general view was summed up in the expression, "they're too thin on the ground". A further point made by some heads (whether it was accurate or not was less relevant in this context than its being *thought* to be the case) was that "advisers don't usually have much management experience", being more often appointed on the basis of their subject expertise than of their seniority in the school hierarchy. So again, a follow-up scheme depending heavily on the participation of advisers would be likely, on the limited evidence so far available, to run into difficulties of both credibility and feasibility.

Two other potential sources of support were mentioned by several heads: namely LEA officers and Chairmen of Governors. The former, particularly regionally-based members of the Authority's staff, were almost invariably seen as helpful, even if in a somewhat limited context – "They're fine on the black and white issues", said one head; "their help has to be asked for rather than given", said another. The latter were also generally viewed as helpful in relation to a circumscribed range of issues – matters to do with parents, the school's relationship with its community, and (on very rare occasions) problems related to the conduct of individual staff members. However, both these sets of contacts already exist, and heads seem to experience no difficulties in activating them when the need arises. Support systems might seek to incorporate them, but would certainly have no need to reinvent them.

A further system of personal contacts appeared to be a particularly supportive one, namely that with other heads – whether or not these happened to be in the near vicinity. The twenty day management course itself was seen as valuable in extending the range of fellow-heads who could be telephoned for specific advice, or even for a general exchange of gossip or shop. "This sort of contact is particularly useful when you're thinking of taking a calculated risk"; "it helps you to find out how near you can sail to the wind, when what you are doing may be justified on moral grounds but is more dubious in strictly legal terms." Even where nearby schools are competing for the same limited pool of entrants, there tends to be a sense of camaraderie rather than competition between the heads – a sense that "we're all in it together". And the reactions of heads from outside the County boundaries are valued because they can often give a fresh slant on a problem, in that their structures and procedures are different. There would seem, then, to be particularly promising opportunities for the support of training programmes in terms of building on and extending the existing networks of heads – a process which has already been initiated by the action learning components of some management courses.

Two main themes emerged from the interviews as reflecting future needs. A number of heads considered that the course had given them a welcome opportunity to stand back and reflect upon their day-to-day experience. They wanted some continuing opportunities to do so: "What is needed is the philosophy of education rather than the nuts and bolts ... a chance to rethink the fundamentals". But a second group of heads adopted a contrasting view, namely that what was needed was a means to implement ideas in practice, and not merely to develop them in theory. Some interviewees commented that they would come back from a session at the management course keen to try out a new idea in their school, only to find that the senior staff were resistant to it. One spoke of the need for "a selling job"; another was prepared to bide his time – "I haven't pushed it yet".

These rival demands – for more scope for reflection, and for more practical help in translating ideas into action – suggest that different heads may be looking for different forms of follow-up support, or at any rate may be starting from discernably different positions.

Preparation and Follow-up in a Newly Established Thirty Day Programme

As nominations to the course were received, participants were sent a letter which welcomed them to membership, gave outline details of the approach and content and signalled four specific tasks.

- course members had to select a personal study topic and let the course organisers know what this was before the course started;
- course members were asked to provide 'a short autobiographical note and statement of the main issues facing yourself and your school over the next few years';
- all course members were to be visited by the director of the course in their own schools before the course began;
- after the course members were expected to write a report on their own personal studies for circulation to other course members.

Preparation

All of the course members were visited in their own schools, and all testified to the value of this – "I've never felt so good about coming on a course as this". "It made me feel much more involved because somebody took the trouble to come and talk to me about it". "It was the big lift-off point". "I felt special". "It stimulated action and gave me some information".

Although two members said they would have preferred an earlier visit (to give even more time for planning and thinking), the others said they thought the timing of the visit was about right. All members sent in biographical details in advance and these were printed by the centre and circulated to all members on arrival. All members chose a personal study topic as asked.

The value which course members placed upon the director's pre-course visits cannot be overstated. All of them saw them as crucial to their commitment to the course. Perhaps the most powerful testimony came from the nominee who was most reluctant to accept a place on the course in the first place. "I don't like professional course goers; I'm very sceptical of in-service courses in general". After he had talked to the director, not only was his apprehension eased but the meeting provided "a lift off on what the course might achieve for me". The juxtaposition of the pre-course visit and the need to choose a personal study topic had increased commitment to the course as a whole and to the need to do some preparatory planning.

The inclusion of a personal study topic did much to create a sense of relevance and engagement. The topics chosen differed widely in terms of the quality and depth of the response exhibited by the different individuals but all were clearly important to them. Some participants were determined to see them through to action in their schools or LEAs: "I shall do my damnedest to make the LEA do something about it if I come up with a scheme I think is worth pursuing". The integration of the personal topic within the course had given them an opportunity to use their own initiative.

Follow-up support

Consideration of what support might be needed after the course was limited by established assumptions about the availability of officers and advisers, and even colleagues in school. "I've got a promise from an adviser to give us an in-service day in school on this topic" (profiling) and "I'd like to persuade the LEA to give me more time – say a day a week – to continue my study".

Probably the most certain shared reaction was the feeling that despite tremendous group solidarity on the course (eight members in total) this was unlikely to be a regular and sustained source of support for the future – "The support I'm finding here is only related to here. I see the possibility of the group coming together again but in between times I don't know". Nevertheless, there were some signs of personal networks developing.

A meeting with the advisers

The course director had written inviting all the nominating advisers to attend a specific session of the course in order to discuss the participants' personal study topics. The plan was for the evening to be divided into two parts. Firstly individual heads would talk over their own projects with their own advisers. Then all of them would come together in a discussion of the opportunities and problems for LEA/Head joint action in implementing any of the ideas being generated. The director's letter of invitation had stressed the centrality of this exercise and had asked advisers to ensure that they were properly represented if they were prevented from attending themselves. In the event, only four LEAs were represented so the evening had to be run entirely as a group discussion. This proved quite fruitful, focussing on the question – how may LEAs, course providers and course members relate in such a way as to enable course members to make best use of course experience?

Each adviser gave a personal response describing the LEA's procedures relating to management training courses. One said his authority operated with a General Adviser attached to each school – "we see him as an extra member of staff" – and by this means identified school and head needs. The participating head from this Authority commented that he agreed "with most of that" but still felt "aggrieved that I don't know why I was put on this course". Another adviser outlined a pattern of headteacher training from induction onwards; heads understood that pattern and all of them who had been on courses were used in training and on committees to spread their expertise around the authority; heads were now being asked to say for themselves when they next wanted a course and of what kind. A third adviser said he had "always tended to ask heads to go on courses expecting that they would contribute as much as they took".

The fourth adviser present made a very different statement:

> "I'm feeling very insecure as to why I'm here rather than my colleague who nominated X to this course. He said it was because he had a rehearsal for his panto but I think it was because he wanted to avoid answering questions as to why X was nominated for this course. I think it was because it was his turn. He is the most senior head in the Authority who hasn't been on a course. The reality is that we don't have an ordered pattern of development. I think I know what X's management problems are but I am not sure and we certainly don't talk to him enough about them. We tend to be bogged down by day to day problems".

This straightforward and detached statement gave rise to a much franker exchange between all concerned about the *lack* of LEA involvement in the process of heads' development, typified by:

> "I don't think either you or I know why we are here, from the Authority's point of view that is, and frankly now I don't want to know".

> "I would have preferred to meet with all the heads in the Authority and hear from the officers why they were nominating me".

> "There is still a need for a greater degree of communication between heads and officers".

This led to a general consensus of all the heads with at least two of the advisers agreeing that before any head went on a course there should be a joint negotiation between the head, the LEA and the provider in order to clarify the purposes of the head's attending the course.

In retrospect it was clear that in most of the LEAs concerned there had been little if any genuine communication about the LEA perspectives of the Head's or the Authority's needs and purposes. Even in the one case where there had been a very close personal exchange between the head and the nominating adviser about the head's chosen topic, the head concerned still remained uncertain of the adviser's (and thus the LEA's) view of the head's and the school's needs.

The same adviser who had spoken candidly before helped bring the evening to a close by interjecting, into a discussion of what forms of support the heads might need in trying to implement any results from their study topics, the question "Can somebody tell me what a study topic is?" He clearly meant to indicate that his LEA had no knowledge of the Head's topic and thus little expectation of readily offering any support. He went on to say that in his view any match between a head's topic and LEA need would be accidental.

At the end of the meeting everyone, heads and advisers alike, seemed genuinely pleased with the form and nature of the discussion. Two advisers voiced the thought that it had been a "rare opportunity to come to grips with the issue of heads' management development in this way". All present clearly valued this opportunity for an open sharing of views between heads and advisers.

References

BALLINGER, E 1984 *Headship in the 80s* Bristol: NDC

BRADDICK, B and CASEY, D 1981 'Developing the forgotten army – learning and the top manager' *Management Education and Development* Vol 12 Part 3 pp 169-180

CASEY, D 1980 'Transfer of learning – there are two separate problems' in J. Beck and C Cox (ed) *Advances in management education* Chichester: Wiley

CASEY, D 1983 'Where action learning fits in' in M. Pedler (ed) *Action learning in practice* Aldershot: Gower

KOLB, D RUBIN, I and MCINTYRE, J 1979 3rd ed *Organisational psychology: an experiential approach* New Jersey: Prentice Hall

MANPOWER SERVICES COMMISSION 1983 *Management self-development: a practical manual for managers and trainers* Sheffield: MSC

REVANS, R 1971 *Developing effective managers* New York: Praeger

Conclusion and Recommendations arising from the Project

Throughout our work we have found it necessary to examine the connections between management training and management development. We make the case for a period of incremental change in order to effect the transition to comprehensive systems of management development.

The briefing meetings and supporting activities arranged through the local Joint Plan are a vital first step. They are important, not only in increasing the effectiveness of existing training, but in encouraging practical discussions between heads, officers and advisers on management development matters. These discussions are in themselves examples of the *'sustained experiences'* which the National Development Centre has argued are necessary to effect the transition. Above all, the local plan must ensure that training programmes are located within a broader perspective of mid-career development.

The core of management development remains the development of each individual and involves the acquisition of new knowledge, skills, attitudes and insights. But this must not be interpreted as a simple transfer from those who know to those who do not, or those who can to those who cannot. Most experienced professionals, reflecting on the formative experiences of their career, recall not their training but the influence of particular individuals and organisations they have worked with, or special projects and assignments they have undertaken. Many heads and senior officers, for example, have spoken to us of the great value to be gained by all who participate in local authority working parties and policy study groups. The most significant management development experiences occur in the context of the organisation, its routines and working relationships. Development is largely conditioned by the quality of the everyday experience; training is best seen as an enhancement of this experience.

The Joint Plan will help to integrate existing training within this broader process of development. But beyond this, opportunities occur in all LEAs to organise some training experiences which will

have a more direct impact on the quality of everyday working relationships. This can be achieved by getting people who need to coordinate their work to come together under the special conditions which training can provide to develop new and more effective ways of undertaking the management tasks which confront them. Training of this kind serves three functions:
- it gives new impetus to selected areas of management which are in need of special attention;
- it improves working relationships, working methods and the collective ability to cope with future problems and priorities;
- it provides the kinds of experiences needed for the transition to effective management development systems.

Recommendations for Consideration by Local Education Authorities

(i) Support for school management should be developed incrementally over the next few years towards effective management development programmes with current management training courses providing the starting point.

(ii) Consideration should be given to the adoption of a two-stage strategy of development at the local level:
immediate action to make the best use of current training provision by consolidating arrangements for effective briefing of participants and the provision of support for subsequent action in the schools;
a medium term policy of experimentation with different forms of training provision designed to connect training more directly to the issues and problems of school management which the heads encounter and in some cases to incorporate management action and management change within the training experience.

(iii) A more conscious allocation of resources, particularly of scarce inspector and officer time, is necessary if heads are to receive adequate support before, during and after management training.

(iv) Authorities, when working with providing institutions or operating in consortia, must ensure that a clear planning framework is established to draw together all the elements of support necessary to ensure an effective and practical outcome to training.

(v) Recruitment must be based unequivocally on open discussions which try to match specific development needs with an appropriate training experience.
(vi) Evaluation of training and the assessment of its effectiveness should take account of the wider framework of support provided.
(vii) The principles and procedures outlined in this report should be assessed for their more general relevance to the new arrangements for in-service education proposed for April 1987.

Recommendations for Consideration by Providing Institutions

(i) The recommendations set out above, require the full cooperation of providing institutions.
(ii) There is a need for close liaison with authorities, individually or in small groups, to ensure that:
courses are designed to meet specifically identified training needs;
the results of LEA briefing discussions are taken into account when negotiating personal study programmes with participants;
an adequate range of supporting activities is provided to help participants make good practical use of their training.

Recommendations for Consideration at the National Level

(i) Nationally funded programmes of management training (such as the one indicated in Circular 1/86) should encourage submissions to be cast within a broader planning framework of preparation and support.
(ii) A proportion of any funding earmarked for management training should be allocated to experimental, or specially designed, programmes focussing directly on specific areas of local policy development and school improvement.
(iii) Assistance and advice should be readily available to LEAs and providing institutions in formulating adequate and realistic plans to link management training and management development.

(iv) Provision should be made to disseminate the major elements of this report and to facilitate the discussion of its recommendations. This might best be initiated by a national conference backed by further regional action.

Reference

GREAT BRITAIN: DEPARTMENT OF EDUCATION AND SCIENCE 1986 *The in-service teacher training grants scheme: arrangements for the academic year 1986-87 and revised arrangements to support GCSE training in the academic year 1985-86* Circular 1/86 London: DES

ANNOTATED BIBLIOGRAPHY:
A Guide to Information and Resources Available to Those Planning Support Activities at the Local Level

This Bibliography is intended as a practical guide, providing useful references for those wishing to plan support activities for heads engaged in training. It is not therefore laid out in the usual alphabetical order. Instead, we set out references for each of the types of activity outlined in Chapters Four and Five. These are:

Support for personal action:

a) self-development workshops;
b) mutual support groups;
c) keeping a professional journal.

Support for corporate action:

a) the action learning set;
b) consultancy;
c) the LEA task group.

The list is annotated on a selective basis, drawing attention to those references we have found to be of particular value. Practical guides and manuals are distinguished from further background reading by an asterisk.

Self-development

ARGYRIS, C & SCHON, D 1974 *Theory in practice: increasing professional effectiveness* London: Jossey Bass

The authors conclude that professional practice is related to the ability of practitioners to become competent in taking action and simultaneously reflecting on this action to learn from it. They assume all 'deliberate human action' to be determined by *theories of action* developed and applied by the individuals concerned. Professional effectiveness consists of acquiring, using and modifying appropriate theories of action. It is the quality of the *theories in use* that governs successful practice in a complex and changing environment. The authors develop the concept through case studies of professional action which enable them to evaluate theories in use and to outline the key factors which determine their effect upon professional performance. They show how performance is undermined by action intended more to ensure personal control of the situation and predictable outcomes than to respond openly to changing circumstances. They then proceed to outline the contribution which training might make to the improvement of performance.

ARGYRIS, C & SCHON, D 1978 *Organizational learning: a theory of action perspective* Reading, Mass: Addison Wesley

The concepts applied to the individual's performance in Argyris and Schon (1974) are here applied to the organisation. The authors conclude that an organisation is a *theory of action* shared amongst its members. The introductory chapter defines and exemplifies the two kinds of learning that can take place within an organisation to prevent entropy: 1) single loop learning, when individuals respond to error by modifying strategies and assumptions within *constant* organisational norms and 2) double loop learning, in which response to error questions the *norms* themselves, to arrive at new norms which are more effectively realisable. In both types of learning the *theory of action* is restructured. Organisational learning must take the form of deutero learning, ie second-order, learning about learning. The case study of the principal exemplifies how to fail to bring about change: both principal and teacher employ *self-sealing theories in use,* resorting to strategies to avoid the dangerous ground of incompatible criteria. A summary of the seven phases of intervention in helping a client to solve a problem is provided.

*AUSTIN, B 1979 *Time the essence – a manager's workbook for using time effectively* London: British Institute of Management.

BLANCHARD, K & JOHNSON, S 1983 *The one-minute manager* London: Fontana.

A best-selling book of practical advice on improving managerial effectiveness. Its recipe for success may be summed up as: 'setting one-minute goals, giving one-minute praisings, and delivering one-minute reprimands'. Written in the style of a fable, it is witty, stimulating, and compulsive reading.

BLANCHARD, K & LORBER, R 1984 *Putting the one-minute manager to work* London: Willow, William Collins.

A companion volume to *The one minute manager,* showing how the three secrets of one minute management (viz: setting one minute goals, giving one minute praisings and delivering one minute reprimands) can be applied on a day to day basis to improve performance. Makes ingenious use of acronyms, e.g. PRICE for Pinpoint, Record, Involve, Coach, Evaluate) to make its points as memorable as possible.

BOYDELL, T 1982 'Development' *Management Education and Development* Vol 13 Part 1 pp10-32
Boydell maps out his understanding of the concept of *development* drawing on a range of theoretical models such as Piaget's stage of development, Maslow's hierarchy of needs, and Kohberg's interpersonal concordance of motives for education, and relates these to Alderfer's ERG (Existence, Relatedness, Growth) model. He concludes that development is 'decreased duality, increased unity', i.e. perceiving things not in terms of their duality, as mutually exclusive opposites, but in terms of their essential unity, since everything in the universe is essentially interrelated. The process of development involves restructuring, hence conflict and crisis. Helping people to develop involves supporting them through the four phases identified by Dewey, either in the context of experiences provided by the trainer, or those encountered in everyday life.

*BOYDELL, T 1985 *The management of self-development: a guide for managers, organisations and institutions* Geneva: ILO.
Written for managers who wish to develop their own potential, this describes 26 proven methods and shows how to use them. Two final chapters suggest ways in which managers can support the self development of others, and guidelines for course providers on how to integrate self development with formal training courses.

BOYDELL, T & PEDLER, M (eds) 1981 *Management self-development: concepts and practices* Farnborough: Gower.
Describes a variety of self development strategies. Each method is described by one of its key exponents, who discusses the concepts and principles involved, and – with the help of case studies – the way in which these principles are applied in his particular approach. The 15 contributions range from established methods like the action learning of Reg Revans to newer approaches such as Leary's 'working with biography' and the computer assisted 'reflective learning' being developed at the London Business School.

BURGOYNE, J BOYDELL, T & PEDLER, M 1978 *Self-development: theory and applications for practitioners* London:

Association of Teachers of Management.
A useful brief introduction to the concept of self development. Defines some of the meanings attached to the concept of self development, describes 13 widely used approaches, and gives practical advice on some of the problems of getting started.

BURGOYNE, J & STUART, R 1976 'The nature, use and acquisition of managerial skills and other attributes' *Personnel Review* Vol 5 No 4, pp19-29
Based on interviews with a substantial number of managers, the authors develop a taxonomy of ten broad categories of skills which appeared to equate with successful managerial performance: situational facts, relevant professional knowledge, sensitivity to events, problem-solving skills, social skills and abilities, emotional resilience, proactivity – an inclination to respond purposefully to events, creativity, mental agility, and balanced learning habits and skills. Using this taxonomy as a basis, the article suggests some of the learning areas to which management development activities should be directed. The research also identified nine major sources of managerial learning, ranked by the managers interviewed in the following order of importance: doing the job, non-company education, living, in-company training, self, doing other jobs, media, parents, innate.

BURGOYNE, J & STUART, R 1977 'Implicit learning theories as determinants of the effect of management development programmes' *Personnel Review* Vol 6 No 2 pp5-14.
Using data from a sample of 14 varied programmes, the researchers identified eight schools of thought on learning theory: conditioning, trait modification, information transfer, cybernetic, cognitive, experiential, social influence and pragmatic, and assessed which learning theory was most appropriate, in terms of learning outcomes, for particular learning areas.

CANNING, R 1984 'Management self-development' *Journal of European Industrial Training* Vol 8 No 1 pp8-11
Describes the self-development approach used within the Housing Corporation, London, as a basis for individual employee training. Defines self development as concerned with the 'how' as well as the 'what' of learning – based on Kolb's learning cycle theory, the discounts transactional analysis model for explanation of failure to learn, and Kolb and Honey/Mumford for diagnosis of preferred learning styles. Concludes by describing the stages of the Housing

Corporation training programme: identifying training needs (through self and others' perception) identifying training goals, and implementing plans through self-development support groups.

*ELLIOTT KEMP, J n.d. *Fostering creativity: a practical guide for group training or self-development* Sheffield: Sheffield City Polytechnic, PAVIC Gems No 18
Provides theoretical material and practical techniques to encourage and improve creative thinking in workshops or by individuals. The exercises have been used in creativity workshops directed by the author with a wide range of participants, including OD trainee consultants, school and college principals, teachers and students. It may be used as part of a taught programme or as a self-development guide.

FINEMAN, S & MCLEAN A J 1984 '"Just tell me what to do" – some reflections on running self-development training programmes' in C Cox and J Beck (eds) *Management development: advances in practice and theory* Chichester: Wiley

*FOOD, DRINK & TOBACCO INDUSTRIAL TRAINING BOARD 1978 *Development at work* Gloucester: FDTITB
A loose-leaf collection of practical activities designed to be put to immediate use by managers in developing the skills and attitudes of their employees. An introductory section provides background information on development theory and advice on the identification of needs, tackling the identified needs, and assessing progress. The main section consists of activities to help identify developmental needs and to give ideas on how to tackle those needs.

*FRANCIS, D & WOODCOCK, M 1982 *Fifty activities for self development* Aldershot: Gower.
Provides 50 short exercises – loose-leaf in a ring binder – for remedying the 11 blockages to successful management described in the companion volume *The unblocked manager*. Each blockage is cross-referenced to some 20 exercises.

HAGUE, H 1977 'Getting self-development to happen' Parts 1 & 2 *Journal of European Industrial Training* Vol 1 No 5 pp24-29 & Vol 1 No 6 pp28-31
Two articles give advice to trainers on introducing self development. Part 1 reassures trainers that they have a role in self-development : as catalysts. They can ensure that the organisational climate is right (eg by demonstrating that mistakes

are allowable, or that people matter) and they can get various types of individuals (eg the high flier, the top manager, the switched off) to accept the need for self development. Part 2 suggests steps which the trainer-as-catalyst must take to get self development started a) at *organisational* level: getting the climate right by, for instance, organising a weekend where people can talk openly without feeling insecure; or suggesting innovations such as changing the reward system, suspending the appraisal system, moulding jobs and structures to fit people instead of vice versa; explaining adult learning theory; and b) at *individual* level: use of self assessment questionnaires and diary-keeping; exposing high fliers to experience of failure, top managers to criticism, earnest plodders to minor, manageable change, the switched-off to removal of their excuses for lethargy followed by demands for action. The catalyst's task can be summed up as showing the need to improve, showing how to improve, and providing an incentive for improving.

HAGUE, H 1979 'Tools for helping self-development' *Journal of European Industrial Training* Vol 2 No 3 pp13-15 & Vol 2 No 5 pp18-21 & Vol 3 No 1 pp25-28

Three articles give practical advice to trainers on the use of tools for promoting self development. Part 1 advises on the use of *projects* for training purposes (emphasising the value of real life projects as opposed to training exercises), the range of difficulty, risk and reward of various types of project, the value of the team project, and the importance of the careful selection of team members. Offers suggestions on how the trainer can maintain a role once the project is under way. Part 2 gives practical hints on *coaching* by the boss, and job rotation – and the role of the trainer in influencing the climate and designing the learning situation. Part 3 advises on on-the-job coaching by the trainer: how to initiate the relationship (eg by self assessment questionnaire), how to apply pressure on the manager to overcome reluctance and inertia and do what deep down he knows he ought to do, and how to provide motivation.

HAGUE, H 1979 'Implications of self-development for the training function' *Journal of European Industrial Training* Vol 3 No 3 pp8-12

*HELLER, H 1985 *Helping schools change* York: University of York, Centre for the Study of Comprehensive Schools

Heller's 'Handbook for leaders in education' does not focus precisely on the process of self-development, being of interest to *all* who would help schools to face the challenge of change. But its principal focus is on internal self-review and it will therefore be of particular interest to headteachers. It offers a range of insights and practical methods of analysis that can be adopted within the school in the process of self-review.

*HENNESSY, J & HUGHES, M 1884 *Self development for women managers* Sheffield: MSC

HODGSON, T 1981 'Stimulating self development' in T Boydell and M Pedler (eds) *Management self-development: concepts and practices* Farnborough: Gower

*HONEY, P & MUMFORD, A 1982 *Manual of learning styles* Maidenhead: Peter Honey.
Explains the theory of the Kolb-based learning styles approach in terms that busy managers can understand and use. Provides a learning styles questionnaire to enable managers to diagnose their own predominant learning style (activist, reflective, theorist or pragmatist), identifies learning activities congruent with the four learning styles, and advises on the use of the learning styles approach by the individual, the boss and the adviser.

*HONEY, P & MUMFORD, A 1983 *Using your learning styles* Maidenhead: Peter Honey.
A booklet written to help the learner select learning activities that suit his style (as revealed by completing the appended Learning Styles Questionnaire, reprinted from the *Manual of learning styles*) and to strengthen that which is currently underdeveloped. For each of the four learning styles a list of activities from which the learner would derive most benefit is provided. There is a section of practical suggestions for developing one's weaker styles.

JAAP, T 1979 *The steps to self-development* London: Human Resource Associates
This is an inspirational little book which will help anyone to achieve the aim of self development. Jaap recognises that most people find it difficult, if not traumatic, to break the mould of habit and extend themselves in new directions, and that they need a structure, involving a carefully graded progression of attainable goals, to keep motivation high and ensure perseverance. The book provides a number of examples of such step-by-step projects which can be easily adapted to fit the personal situation of the reader.

JUCH, A 1979 'Development within the organisation' *Management Education and Development* Vol 10 No 1 Spring

KENT, R 1982 'Transfer of training without the boss' *Journal of European Industrial Training* Vol 6 No 3 pp17-19
Recommends two techniques – self-monitoring, and the follow-up meeting – as effective means of reinforcing on-the-job application of skills learned on a training course, on the grounds that trainees are more highly motivated by being given responsibility for their own development than by external reinforcement from the boss.

KOLB, D 1974 'On management and the learning process' in D Kolb, I Rubin & J McIntyre (eds) 1974 (3rd ed) *Organisational psychology: a book of readings* New Jersey: Prentice Hall pp27-40
Kolb develops an experiential learning model to explain how managers and professionals learn and develop. This provides an important conceptual framework for self-development activities. Chapter 5 provides a description of the model.

KOLB, D & BOYATZIS, R 1974 'Goal setting and self directed behaviour change' in Kolb et al (eds) 1974 pp 349-369
Discusses how to help someone achieve a behavioural change – based on Kolb's *experiential learning model* described in a previous chapter – through goal setting, imported from Rogerian client-centred therapy. After describing an experiment to identify the characteristics of the goal setting process a cybernetic model of behaviour change and helping interventions is offered – tentatively.

KOLB, D & FRY, R 1975 'Towards an applied theory of experiential learning' in C Cooper (ed) 1975 *Theories of group processes* Chichester: Wiley
This is another account of Kolb's work on the experiential learning model and learning style inventory, set in the context of other work in this field.

KOLB, D & PLOVNIVK, M 1977 'The experiential learning theory of career development' in J van Maanen (ed) 1977 *Organisational careers: some new perspectives* Chichester: Wiley

LEARY, M 1981 'Working with biography' in T Boydell and M Pedler (eds) *Management self-development: concepts and practices* Farnborough: Gower

LEARY, M 1984 'Some thinking exercises on inner and outer development' *Management Education and Development* Vol 15 Part 1 pp58-61

*LEIGH, A 1983 *Decisions, decisions : a practical management

guide to problem-solving and decision-making London: Institute of Personnel Management (IPM)
A systematic guide through the phases of problem-solving and decision-making, including implementation. Each chapter covers one aspect of the process which leads to a decision, the methods one can use – including creativity, intuition, groups, decision-analysis – and how to cope with stress.

*LEIGH, A 1984 *Twenty ways to manage better* London: Institute of Personnel Management (IPM)
Distils into 20 short chapters the essential practical advice for improving management skills. Each chapter deals, simply and concisely, with a different topic: setting objectives, recruitment and selection, appraisal and review, coaching, problem people, negotiating, facts from figures, employee communications, verbal presentations, listening, better reading, small information systems, coping with failure, project management, the problem list, new technology. Evaluated bibliography. Compulsive reading, and useful as a basic recipe book to be kept at hand. Many invaluable check lists.

*LOCAL GOVERNMENT TRAINING BOARD 1977 *Could you be a better manager?* Luton: LGTB

*LOCAL GOVERNMENT TRAINING BOARD 1984 *First line managers in local government: a self help management development programme* Bristol: University of Bristol, School for Advanced Urban Studies/School of Applied Social Studies

*LOCAL GOVERNMENT TRAINING BOARD 1984 *The effective manager: a resource handbook* Luton: LGTB
A loose-leaf ring file of practical exercises for improving management skills. Each of the five sections first sets out its key issues on white pages and then provides a series of exercises on green pages.

*MANPOWER SERVICES COMMISSION 1983 *Management self-development: a practical manual for managers and trainers* Sheffield: MSC.
Generally found to be the most useful of the training manuals. An introductory section of guide notes for trainers gives advice on the key issues facing a trainer in the early stages of promoting and facilitating self-development in an organisation. The main section consists of 75 exercises compiled from a wide range of

acknowledged sources. The exercises cover the following aspects of self-development: self-assessment (personal, at work, and in relationships); job/career/lifeplanning; management activities; leadership/management style; organisational climate; roles/ relationships; power/authority/motivation; learning; general self-development issues; training skills. An indication is given against each item as to whether it is designed for individual or group use or optionally for either. The loose leaf format facilitates distribution.

MOLANDER, C F & WALTON, D 1984 'Getting management development started: the manager as trainer' in C Cox and J Beck (eds) *Management development: advances in practice and theory* Chichester: Wiley

MUMFORD, A 1979 'Self-development – flavour of the month' *Journal of European Industrial Training* Vol 3 No 3 pp13-15
Warns against the overenthusiastic espousal of the self development approach until it has been satisfactorily defined, its objectives clarified and its risks recognized. He offers the definition: 'the process of improving effectiveness through a planned learning experience', and gives some examples of clear objectives and of some of the functions of the self development adviser.

PEDLER, M 1982 'Action learning and self development: the knight and the monk' *Management Education and Development* Vol 15 Part 1 1984 pp55-58
Uses the symbols of the active, combatant knight and the meditating, pacific monk to illustrate the apparently dichotomous, but in fact essentially symbiotic, relationship between action learning and self development.

PEDLER, M 1982 'Support groups for management self-development' *Training Officer* Jan/Feb pp7-12
This paper consists of four parts. The first part discusses the move towards self-development approaches to education and training. The second suggests that managerial competencies and skills generally come about not through formal training but as a result of self-development processes. Following this is a brief description of management self-development – what it is and what it means in practice. The final section of the paper discusses the need for support in the self development process and suggests that support groups of learning communities go some way towards meeting this need.

PEDLER, M 1982 'Supporting managment self-development' *Journal of Management Development* Vol 1 No 3 pp30-42

PEDLER, M 1983 'What is management self-development' in B Taylor & G Lippitt (eds) *A Handbook of management development* Maidenhead: McGraw Hill

PEDLER, M 1985 *Managing self development* Paper provided by the author (Mimeo, 7pp) Sheffield: Sheffield City Polytechnic, Dept of Management Studies

This short paper introduces the idea of self-development to bankers. It explains what self development is, using the slogan 'managing ME first' to put over the 'inside-out' approach which is the essence of self-development: manage yourself, and you will be able to manage other people; the skills of managing others cannot just be grafted on to you. Pedler explains the Kolb learning cycle model and the 'whole person' approach which are integral to self-development. He concludes by discussing how self-development can be resourced within the organisation, and what the role of the trainer is in self-development.

PEDLER, M 1985 'Self-development – with a little help from your friends' *Training Officer* July pp196-199

Reports on three years' experience in helping to initiate and support mutual support groups for promoting management self-development in a variety of organisations. In particular it provides guidelines for setting up and managing a self-development group, breaking the process down into eight phases: setting up and recruiting; getting started – the first meeting; choosing a focus; decision-making; maintaining energy and commitment; helpful actions in groups; reviewing progress; and closing down. For each phase Pedler suggests a few exercises to help participants to develop as a group.

PEDLER, M & BOYDELL, T 1979 *Self-development bibliography* Bradford: MCB Publishers

PEDLER, M & BOYDELL, T 1981 'What is self-development?' in T Boydell and M Pedler (eds) *Management self-development: concepts and practices* Farnborough: Gower

A brief summary of the way these two leading exponents of self-development understood the concept in 1981.

PEDLER, M & BOYDELL, T 1984 *The role of the trainer in self development* Paper given at a seminar for civil service training managers, Sept 5 1984 Sheffield: Sheffield City Polytechnic, Dept of Management Studies

PEDLER, M & BOYDELL, T 1985 *Managing yourself* London: Fontana

PEDLER, M BOYDELL, T LEARY, M CARLISLE, J & CRANWELL, B 1984 *Self-development groups for managers* Sheffield: MSC

A report summarising the findings of a mainly MSC funded programme assessing the effectiveness of self-development groups for managers. The summary concentrates on the initiation, establishment and maintenance of groups (giving lots of practical advice) rather than on the detail of running groups. Part 2 consists of detailed case studies of various groups run during the life of the project (1980-2): the Bradford Metropolitan District Council self-development and biography groups, self-development groups in a multi-national pharmaceutical company, pseudonymed Islay, the Sheffield Managing Directors' Group, the Sheffield Employment Initiatives group, and the Geest Organisation groups.

*PEDLER, M BURGOYNE, J & BOYDELL, T 1978 *A manager's guide to self-development* Maidenhead: McGraw Hill

Explains the concept of self-development and provides a collection of exercises organised under topic headings, e.g. keeping a journal, use of time, etc.

PHILLIPS, A 1983 'Management self-development – reaping the benefit of self-managed learning' *BACIE Journal* Vol 38 No 3 May/June pp87-90

Describes the background and scope of the MSC *Management self-development manual*, and the seminars organised by BACIE to coach delegates in the use of the manual.

*PFEIFFER, J & JONES, J (eds) 1969, 1970, 1971, 1973, 1975 and 1977 respectively *A handbook of structured exercises Vols I-VI* La Jolla: University Associates

One of the best-known sources of structured exercises, most of which are not perhaps strictly self-development, but are closely related.

RICHARDSON, J & BENNETT, B 1984 'Applying learning techniques to on-the-job development' *Journal of European Industrial Training* Vol 8 Nos 1,3 & 4 pp3-7, 5-10 and 3-7 respectively

Three articles provide an interesting account of an off-the-job training programme based specifically on the Kolb-based analysis of the participants' style of learning, with support for its application to practical situations.

STUART, R 1984 'Maximising managers' day-to-day learning: frameworks for the practice of learning interventions' in C Cox and J Beck (eds) *Management development: advances in practice and theory* Chichester: Wiley

Establishes the need for interventions to help managers maximise their development of all four of the skills involved in the Kolb learning cycle. Sets out in matrix form various frameworks to help the 'learning consultant' to understand the nature of individuals' learning problems (intrinsic and extrinsic blocks and barriers) and to identify appropriate interventions to reduce these problems. Five basic types of learning intervention roles are identified (drawing on Blake and Mouton's (1976) five styles of consultative activity) viz: acceptant, catalytic, confrontational, prescriptive and theory/principle based, and relates these (with a summary in table form) to the various types of learning problems.

STUART, R & BURGOYNE, J 1977 'The learning goals and outcomes of management development programmes' *Personnel Review* Vol 6 No 1 pp5-16

Based on an investigation of a range of management development programmes an overall picture is built up of the types of skills learning which was in fact resulting from current management development activities. This picture is compared with that of the intended learning goals.

STUART, R & BURGOYNE, J 1977 'Teaching and training skills for translating learning theory into practice in management development programmes' *Personnel Review* Vol 6 No 3 pp39-47

Begins with a matrix presenting the relationships between the acquisition of managerial skills, the learning theories which trainers commonly considered appropriate for enhancing particular skills, and the learning theories which were found to be most strongly associated with high learning *outcomes* on a particular skill, whether or not these outcomes were intended. The paper then considers how these data might be used to facilitate decision-making in the design of management development programmes.

TEMPORAL, P 1978 'The nature of non-contrived learning and its implications for management development' *Management*

Education and Development Vol 9 Reprinted in P Temporal and T Boydell 1981 *Helping managers to learn* Sheffield: Sheffield City Polytechnic, Dept. of Management Studies
After identifying the main non-contrived sources of learning (those identified by Burgoyne and Stuart 1976, and also coaching and the organisational climate) Temporal categorises five main types of internal block to learning, viz: perceptual, cultural, emotional-motivational, intellectual, and expressive. The effects of these blocks on a manager's approach to non-contrived learning situations are set out in table form.

TEMPORAL, P 1981 'Creating the climate for self-development' in T. Boydell and M. Pedler (eds) *Management development : concepts and practices* Farnborough: Gower

TEMPORAL, P & BOYDELL, T 1977 'Barriers to Learning' *BACIE Journal* October pp154-5. Reprinted in P Temporal and T Boydell 1981 *Helping managers to learn* Sheffield: Sheffield City Polytechnic, Department of Management Studies
Outlines the nature of barriers or blocks to learning – both internal, and external i.e. resulting from the organisational or learning climate – describes how they affect people, and suggests some ways in which they might be overcome.

TEMPORAL, P 1984 'Helping self-development to happen' in C Cox and J Beck (eds) *Management development: advances in practice and theory* Chichester: Wiley

TEMPORAL, P & BOYDELL, T 1981 *Helping managers to learn* Sheffield: Sheffield City Polytechnic, Dept of Management Studies, Occasional Paper No 1
A quick way in to recent work on managerial skills and qualities (Pedler et al), learning blocks (Temporal et al) and organisation climate (Knowles). This short report summarises the 3-year research and development programme undertaken by Boydell et al at Sheffield Polytechnic. The programme selected from the literature the most useful concepts and practical ideas on skills, learning blocks and organisational climate to provide a basis for developing resources to help managers maximise their self-development. Examples of the resources developed – an instrument for measuring learning climate and instruments to diagnose learning blocks – are included.

WINKLESS, T & BOYDELL, T 1981 'Self development groups' in

T Boydell and M Pedler (eds) *Management self-development: concepts and practices* Farnborough: Gower
Describes the experience of self-development groups within the Geest organisation – including some self evaluations from participants. Raises the issue of whether the organisational climate is supportive, or did the success of those groups rest on the facilitator's skill?

*WOODCOCK, M & FRANCIS, D 1982 *The unblocked manager* Aldershot: Gower
Begins by providing a set of 110 questions and a grid sheet to enable a manager to diagnose his own particular blockages. The questions are structured around 11 key blockage concepts: self management incompetence; unclear personal values; unclear personal goals; stunted personal development; inadequate problem-solving skills; low creativity; low influence; lack of managerial insight; poor supervisory skills; low trainer capability; low team-building capacity. The main part of the book consists of 11 essays, each describing one of the blockages under several headings, with suggestions for remedying it. The book concludes with a short guide to practical activities for remedying the blockages. A fuller set of activities is provided in the complementary publication *Fifty activities for self development*.

Mutual support groups

BOUD, D & McDONALD, R 1981 *Educational development through consultancy* Guildford: University of Surrey, Society for Research into Higher Education.
See under consultancy.

*BOYDELL, T 1985 *Management self-development* Geneva: ILO
Chapter 8, How other people can help your self-development, includes among its suggestions working with a partner, and mutual support groups of various kinds, and Chapters 9 and 10 on promoting self-development within an organisation also mention these techniques.

BUCKLEY, J 1985 'How training needs are being met: France' in *The training of secondary school heads in Western Europe* Windsor: NFER-Nelson
The French national training scheme for prospective heads includes

the linking of a new head to an experienced neighbour, and regional meetings of heads in a district to provide mutual support.

BURGOYNE, J, BOYDELL, T & PEDLER, M 1978 *Self-development: theory and applications for practitioners* London: Association of Teachers of Management
The central section of practical suggestions for self development includes a brief but succinct description of the "learning community" (defined as a group of people who come together to meet specific and unique learning needs, and to share resources and skills), of its objectives, and of the 5-stage process model characteristic of the learning community.

DEAN, J 1981 'Advisory service' in E Henderson and G Perry (eds) *Change and development in schools* Maidenhead: McGraw Hill
Peer group assessment and the support of colleagues formed an essential element of the Surrey management training course for heads described in this case study.

*ELLIOTT-KEMP, J 1982 *Managing organisational change: a practitioner's guide* Sheffield: Sheffield City Polytechnic, Department of Education Services, PAVIC Gems No 14
Among the methods advocated by Elliot-Kemp is that of peer counselling.

ESP, D 1980 *The selection and training of headteachers in Sweden* Report on the author's AEC Trust Fellowship study visit. Taunton: Somerset Education Committee
The national compulsory School Leader Education (SLE) programme intends that all school leaders in a kommun will attend simultaneously, to facilitate (non-compulsory) meetings of study-circles in the kommun.

GARNHAM, A 1981 'Professional partnership in practice: the South West INSET Committee' in C Donoughue et al (eds) *In-service: the teacher and the school* London: Kogan Page/OU
Describes the setting up of a professional partnership group concerned with the management of INSET at regional level. It comprised 4 LEA representatives (Avon, Gloucestershire, Somerset and Wiltshire), 5 representatives of the teacher education institutes, 5 teachers (representatives of the Unions), and 1 HMI. It is a consultative body, not an executive one, with no legal base. Its concern is to influence LEAs, providers and teachers, and to establish priorities and new approaches in INSET. The

development of a climate of partnership has helped to break down the often wasteful and competitive situation.

HAMILTON, E 1985 *Professional partners* (publicity brochure) Columbia, Maryland: Hamilton Associates

HARRI-AUGSTEIN, S & THOMAS, L 1981 'Learning conversations' in T Boydell and M Pedler (eds) *Management self-development: concepts and practices* Farnborough: Gower
Starting from the premise that learning to learn consists in an ability to converse with oneself about the process of learning, this article introduces a number of learning conversation techniques developed in the last ten years at the Centre for the Study of Human Learning at Brunel University, and then looks at the implications for trainers.

HELLER, H 1982 'Management development for headteachers' in H Gray (ed) *The management of educational institutions: theory, research and consultancy* Lewes: Falmer Press
Provides an example of the way one LEA – Cleveland – went about providing management training for its heads in the period 1974-82, trying new and sometimes risky ideas and developing and modifying courses in the light of experience, feedback from participants, and stimulation and support from local industry (especially ICI). Of particular interest is the success of the 'Norton Hardwick Group' – a multi professional support group based at ICI's management training centre which helped to shape the early progress of training efforts, and also the evolution of a core group of heads and advisers as course leaders and facilitators.

HERON, J 1974 *The concept of a peer learning community* Human Potential Research Project, Guildford: University of Surrey, Centre for Adult Education

HERON, J 1979 *Peer review audit* University of London, British Post-graduate Medical Federation

HERON, J 1981 'Self and peer assessment' in T Boydell and M Pedler (eds) *Management self-development: concepts and practices* Farnborough: Gower
Heron describes the seven stages of his peer review audit and illustrates them with case material.

HERON, J 1981 'Experiential research methodology' and 'Philosophical basis for a new paradigm' in P. Reason and J. Rowan (eds) *Human inquiry: a sourcebook of new paradigm research* Chichester: Wiley

KIRSCHENBAUM, H & GLASER, B 1978 *Developing support groups* La Jolla: University Associates

McINTOSH, M 1985 *Towards a management development policy for headteachers in secondary schools: a study of heads, tasks and resources* Bristol: University of Bristol, NDC, Occasional Paper No 2

Reviews management development initiatives by some LEAs mentioning the WISH scheme's aim to create networks of mutual support between headteachers, and the NWEMC's coordinated mutual support group of 16 heads in Salford LEA. The concluding list of recommendations includes the establishment of networks of heads who would visit each others' schools to examine how they approach a common problem.

*OLDROYD, D SMITH, K & LEE, J 1984 *School-based staff development activities: a handbook for secondary schools* York: Longman for Schools Council pp166-170

Describes an example of mutual support groups for teachers. Three self-regulating staff development groups were set up at a school as a result of a short course on pupil motivation, and their success or otherwise is evaluated at the end of term by the participants of the three groups.

PEDLER, M 1981 'Developing the learning community' in T Boydell & M Pedler (eds) *Management self-development: concepts and practices* Farnborough: Gower

PEDLER, M 1982 'Support groups for management self-development' *Training Officer* Jan/Feb pp7-12

The final section of this paper discusses the need for support in the self-development process and suggests that support groups of learning communities go some way towards meeting this need. See under self-development.

PEDLER, M 1985 'Self-development – with a little help from your friends' *Training Officer* July pp196-199

Gives advice on how to initiate and manage mutual support groups for promoting management self-development. See under self-development.

PEDLER, M BOYDELL, T LEARY, M CARLISLE, J & CRANWELL, B 1984 *Self-development groups for managers* Sheffield: MSC
See under Self-development.

POWELL, J P 1985 'Autobiographical learning' in D Boud, R Keogh and D Walker (eds) *Reflection: turning experience into learning* London: Kogan Page
See under journal.

SCHMUCK, R 1978 'Peer consultation for school improvement' in C Cooper and C Alderfer (eds) *Advances in experiential social processes* London: Wiley
See under consultancy.

WEEKS, J 1983 *The professional development of secondary heads* Bristol: Avon Education Department
As a result of his assessment of the heads' training provision in the Northern Sub-Region of the SW Inset Committee, Weeks recommended a one-term training module in which a central feature would be a programme of visits by the 16 participating heads to each others' schools in order to discuss and appraise each others' management techniques and styles.

WOODS, T L 1973 'The study group: a mechanism for continuing education and professional self-development' *Clinical Social Work Journal* Vol 2 No 2
There is something of a tradition for support groups or study groups in psychiatry and social work which has lessons for management self-development.

Keeping a professional journal

ABBS, P 1974 *Autobiography in education* London: Heinemann
Advocates the value of autobiographical accounts for recreating and reflecting on the personal past, and to promote peer group discussion and support, in teacher training.

BARNES, P 1981 *Education through autobiography* Milton Keynes: Open University
Part of the OU E200 course, this aims to help students construct their own educational autobiography as an aid to understanding the range of experiences which contributes to an individual's development.

BOYDELL, T 1985 *The management of self development: a guide for managers, organisations and institutions* Geneva: ILO
In a book full of practical suggestions for self-development, there are two specific, and very brief, references on keeping a journal

(p69 and p204), but much of the advice on reflection given in various chapters is, of course, pertinent.

BUTLER, S 1982 'Assessing the journal : an exercise in self-evaluation' *English Quarterly* Vol 14 No 4 pp75-83

CHRISTENSEN, R 1981 '"Dear diary": a learning tool for adults' *Lifelong learning: the adult years* Vol 5 No 2 pp4-5 and 31

KOLB, D RUBIN, I & MCINTYRE, J (eds) 1974 (3rd ed) *Organisational psychology: a book of readings* New Jersey: Prentice Hall

*MANPOWER SERVICES COMMISSION 1983 *Management self-development: a practical manual for managers and trainers* Sheffield: MSC
One of the activities (No 39) provided in this manual is on keeping a professional journal, and provides a step-by-step framework.

MILLS, C W 1970 *The sociological imagination* Harmondsworth: Penguin
The key section of this book in the context of journal writing is the appendix "on individual craftsmanship". Mills gives a brief but powerful and practical account of the way he goes about his work as a social scientist. It is of direct interest to *anyone* intending to keep a journal.

*PEDLER, M BURGOYNE, J & BOYDELL, T 1978 *A manager's guide to self-development* Maidenhead: McGraw Hill
Recommends (pp82-86) keeping a journal as an aid to reflection, and suggests using the left hand page to report factually on events, and the right hand page to record personal responses to what happened, gradually including the dimensions of evaluation of that response and assessing what has been learnt from the process of keeping a journal.

PINAR, W & GRUMET, M 1976 *Toward a poor curriculum* Dubuque, Iowa: Kendall/Hunt Publishing
A reaction against the traditional focus on the external curriculum in favour of focusing on the inner reality of the learning experiences of individuals. In the learning procedure advocated by Pinar and Grumet, autobiographical writings and journal entries are used not so much to analyse the past as to provide, by means of the techniques of free association and peer group comment, a source of energy and direction for future development.

POWELL, J P 1985 'Autobiographical learning' in D Boud, R Keogh and D Walker (eds) *Reflection: turning experience into learning* London: Kogan Page
Not specifically about journal keeping, but what it says about autobiographical writing as an aid to reconstructing experience in order to reflect on it – and gain the insights and criticisms of tutor and peers – is of obvious relevance.

RAINER, T 1980 *The new diary* London: Angus and Robertson
Offers practical advice on keeping a diary, including writing for catharsis, describing events, and free writing from intuition. Seven techniques are singled out: the use of a list, construction of portraits, sketching maps of consciousness, use of guided imagery, seeing things from an altered point of view, writing unsent letters, and imaginary dialogues with others.

SCHON, D 1983 *The reflective practitioner* London: Temple Smith
Although this work is not of direct relevance to journal writing it offers a valuable analysis of the importance of "reflection in action" in professional and managerial life.

STANSBURY, D 1980 'The record of personal experience' in T Burgess and E Adams (eds) *Outcomes of education* London: Macmillan

WALKER, D 1985 'Writing and reflection' in D Boud, R Keogh and D Walker (eds) *Reflection: turning experience into learning* London: Kogan Page
Based on the experience of using journal keeping as a teaching method in a one year full time leadership development programme, Walker offers some very practical suggestions for keeping a journal and for introducing the exercise to course participants, as well as an analysis of its value as an aid to reflection.

WOLF, J F 1980 'Experiential learning in professional education: concept and tools' *New directions in experiential learning* Vol 8 pp17-26

Action Learning

BECK, J & COX, C (eds) 1980 *Advances in management education* Chichester: Wiley

BERGER, M & NIXON, B 1981 'Management development that works' *Journal of European Industrial Training* Vol 5 No 3 pp2-7

Describes a Sun Alliance project which achieved a high level of personal learning and practical organisational improvements. The overall conclusion was that it is essential for training programmes to be integrated with the job requirements and organisational demands. Unless there are specific learning goals, and a close connection between training and work setting, the transfer of learning is unlikely. The article proposes a framework for designing training activities and integrating them into the work setting, describes the implementation of such a framework in the Sun Alliance programme, and draws out the key learning points for trainers which emerge from the success of this programme.

BODDY, D 1979 'Some lessons from an action learning programme' *Journal of European Industrial Training* Vol 3 No 3 pp17-21
Outlines a number of practical lessons and issues relating to action learning which emerged in the course of a programme undertaken by managers of four GEC companies in Scotland.

BODDY, D 1981 'Putting action learning into action' *Journal of European Industrial Training* Vol 5 No 5 pp1-20
Draws on the experience of several action learning programmes to highlight the practical issues involved. Outlines the basic ideas of action learning, and how these can contribute to management development. Considers the main areas of choice in programme design, viz, the project, roles, and the group meetings. Concludes by considering the implications of the issues raised for the trainer, and offering some guidelines on the way these can be handled.

BOOT, R & REYNOLDS, M 1984 'Rethinking experience-based events' in C Cox and J Beck (eds) *Management development: advances in practice and theory* Chichester: Wiley

BOUD, D KEOGH, R & WALKER, D (eds) 1985 *Reflection: turning experience into learning* London: Kogan Page
Grounded in Kolb's experiential learning model, this book advocates various methods to facilitate *reflection* as the key element in converting experience into learning. The ten articles – by practitioners in the professional or spiritual development of adults – present a range of ideas, methods and approaches which will help both providers of training and those involved in self-development, to facilitate the process of reflection. Includes articles on debriefing, learning conversations, peer group counselling (J Heron) and journal keeping (by J Powell and D Walker). See under mutual

support groups and professional journal.

BRADDICK, B & CASEY, D 1981 'Developing the forgotten army – learning and the top manager' *Management Education and Development* Vol 12 Part 3 pp169-180
Describes the experience of an action learning set for top managers in which participants ended up reframing their personal lives instead of how they ran their companies. A normal action learning set moves from cognitive reporting through action to the largely emotional activity of offering support or exerting pressure – with the set adviser's meta-questions performing the iconoclastic role of smashing the learner's habitual frames and thus forcing him to reframe (see Harries' (1981) model of a Maslow-type hierarchy of activities). This set moved from reporting to support / pressure, but work-related activity was largely replaced by reflection on life style, and the emotional pressures were deeply exhausting. The organisers warn that note must be taken of the life phase of participants when setting up an action learning set.

CASEY, D 1976 'The emerging role of set adviser in action learning programmes' *Journal of European Training* Vol 5 No 3
Explains what an 'action learning set' is, and then outlines the role of the set adviser, and the personal characteristics and skills needed by the set adviser. Good teachers are likely to possess the personal characteristics needed, but will have to accept that some of their skills will be redundant, and that they will have to develop others.

CASEY, D 1978 'Project training for managers – the underlying paradox' *Journal of European Industrial Training* Vol 2 No 5 pp3-6
Argues that the value of the project for training lies not in the project itself, but in learning about the processes involved in implementing a management project: 1) the role of the external consultant; 2) organisation change processes; 3) interpersonal processes – for which an action learning set of managers with projects provides an appropriate learning area. This wider view of the value of project training opens up a new scale of opportunity for the manager's development, ranging from the particular achievement of the project at one end, through the development of generalising/synthesising abilities to reframing of his whole life as well as his work at the other end.

CASEY, D 1980 'Transfer of learning – there are two separate problems' in J Beck & C Cox (eds) *Advances in management education* Chichester: Wiley

After exposing the two problems of learning transfer in management education 1) the gap between course and work, and 2) the fact that management is a whole-person activity, not just intellectual, Revans' solution is described, viz: action learning sets, in which managers learn with and from each other, transferring knowledge gained from one whole-person work experience to another through cognitive interpolation. The second part of the article describes one company's attempts to put these ideas into practice: using *application groups* (small groups of managers and facilitators) in which managers can share the difficulties of application of management skills to the sequence of work experiences undertaken for the course.

CASEY, D 1983 'Where action learning fits in' in M Pedler (ed) *Action learning in practice* Aldershot: Gower

Argues that action learning sets provide the ideal conditions for learning: 1) involvement of the whole person in real life activity; 2) time to reflect; 3) deep personal ownership of the projected achievement. Trainers can accelerate and catalyse the learning processes, but they must start where the learner is, not offer something from outside. Concludes with practical hints to trainers for implementing some of the basic principles of action learning.

CASEY, D & HASTINGS, C 1983 'Day release for chief executives' *Personnel Management* June

CASEY, D & PEARCE, D 1977 *More than management development: action learning at the GEC* Farnborough: Gower

EVERARD, K 1982 *Management in comprehensive schools – what can be learned from industry?* York: University of York, Centre for the Study of Comprehensive Schools

To complement the Hughes (1981) report on the provision of courses in educational management by the *public sector*, this report reviews the wealth of management training experience available in *industry* which could contribute to the development of school management training.

HARRIES, J 1981 'The role of action learning set advisers' *Training* Vol 7 No 2 pp7-8

Provides a model of the Maslow type hierarchy of activities – proceeding from cognitive reporting through a short repeat cycle of action to emotional support or pressure – to represent the process of learning which takes place in action sets.

HUCZYNSKI, A 1978 'Approaches to the problem of learning transfer' *Journal of European Industrial Training* Vol 2 No 1 pp26-29
Offers practical advice to trainers on the development of skills *on the course* which can be applied back on the job. Describes five activities (based on ideas in Miles (1959) *Learning to work in groups: a programme guide for educational leaders*) viz: 1) the theory of application sessions; 2) problem centred groups; 3) situational diagnosis; 4) intervisitation; 5) reporting session – in which participants of a previous course report on their implementation back on the job of ideas learned on the course.

JONES, R & WOODCOCK, R 1981 'Diagnostic skills, training and action learning' *Journal of European Industrial Training* Vol 5 No 4 pp14-16
Describes an action learning set, selected by Allied Breweries as the best means of training managers in diagnostic skills to allow greater plant utilisation. The programme was considered successful not only in its development of the participants' diagnostic skills but in the development of their general managerial style and ability to pass on their training to their staffs.

LESSEM, R 1984 'The gestalt of action learning' in C Cox and J Beck (eds) *Management development: advances in practice and theory* Chichester: Wiley

MACNAMARA, M & WEEKES, W 1982 'The action learning model of experiential learning for developing managers' *Human Relations* Vol 35 No 10 pp879-902
Collates a theoretical background for Revans' action learning model of management education. It relates the learning processes that occur in the action learning model to the basic concepts of group dynamics proposed by Bion (1961) *Experiences in groups* London: Tavistock. Action learning offers education that is active, experience based, problem oriented, continuous, supportive, modified by feedback, highly motivated, and, in addition, has the ability to harness the unconscious forces of group symbiosis. It is the reinforcement of this symbiotic effect by the group leader or set adviser which is the distinctive characteristic of the action learning model.

MARGERISON, C 1978 'Action research and action learning in management education' *Journal of European Industrial Training* Vol 2 No 6 pp22-25

This article, written in 1978, illustrates how resistant training institutions still were to the ideas of action learning propounded in the 60s and earlier by Dewey, Revans, Schein and others. Margerison calls for management training which uses the manager's work situation as the context for learning to ensure transfer of learning to the real-life situation after the course. He predicts that the personal development of the manager, improved communication with others within and outside the organisation, and training set in the context of organisation development, will be the main focus of training activity in the future. He has been proved right.

PEDLER, M 1981 *The diffusion of action learning* Sheffield: Sheffield City Polytechnic, Dept of Management Studies
A report of a joint project by Sheffield and Teesside Polytechnics, funded by the Training Services Division of the MSC. Describes the initiation of two action learning sets, in South and North Yorkshire respectively. The report consists of personal accounts of their experience by the individual members of the two action learning sets.

PEDLER, M 1982 'Action learning and self development: the knight and the monk' *Management Education and Development* Vol 15 Part 1 1984 pp55-58
See under self-development.

PEDLER, M 1983 *Action learning in practice* Aldershot: Gower

REVANS, R 1971 *Developing effective managers* New York: Praeger

REVANS, R 1977 'An action learning trust' *Journal of European Industrial Training* Vol 1 No 1 pp2-5

REVANS, R 1980 *Action learning* London: Blond & Briggs

REVANS, R 1981 'Action learning and the development of the self' in T Boydell & M Pedler (eds) *Management self development: concepts and practices* Farnborough: Gower pp209-222
Castigates our educational system which focuses on knowing about things rather than mastery over them. Then shows – with many literary references – how action learning integrates knowing and doing. Warns that action learning involves shock, loss of security, exchanging the comfort of the familiar for the open wilderness, but only thus is self development made possible and programmed knowledge replaced by creativity.

REVANS, R 1982 'Action learning: its origins and nature' *Higher Education Review* Vol 15 No 1 pp20-28
Describes the first action learning programme ever undertaken – in the coal mining industry – when 22 managers from pits all over the country met regularly over three years to identify, and work at solving, their problems, thus forming a community of self development. The three main factors to be noted from this programme are: 1) the action learning was undertaken to solve a real problem, not as a teaching instrument; 2) the learning consisted in new perceptions and changed interpretations rather than fresh data; and 3) the programme attacked problems, not puzzles (ie solutions did not already exist). Designers of action learning programmes must ensure that all that goes on in the set has its counterpart in the field of action. *Talking about action* must not be confused with *action* itself.

REVANS, R 1982 *The origins and growth of action learning* Bromley : Chartwell Bratt

REVANS, R 1983 *The ABC of action learning* Bromley : Chartwell Bratt
A symposium of pieces which together provide a condensed summary of the main ideas worked out by Revans in the course of his 40 years' devotion to the promotion of action learning. The book sets out a list of the twenty "inalienable assumptions" of action learning, gives examples of some operational forms assumed by action learning programmes, suggests how action learning programmes can help to develop managers' strengths and correct their frailties, analyses the responses of top managers in Belgium, discusses the (ancient) philosophy of action learning, describes a few examples of action learning programmes, discriminates between action learning and traditional methods, and draws conclusions from experiences world-wide of launching action learning. Concludes with a full bibliography contributed by the Action Learning Trust.

REVANS, R 1983 'Action learning' 4 articles in *Management Development* Vol 21 Nos 1-4
Four articles describe the process of action learning, covering the following aspects: its terms and character; the skills of diagnosis; the forces of achievement, or getting it done; and the cure is started.

REVANS, R 1984 *The sequence of managerial achievement*

Bradford: MCB Publications
This book, by the developer of action learning, is a collection of articles and papers by the author showing what action learning means to business and industry. They explore the theory and practice of action learning, describing how it works in various organisations.

SMITH, D 1983 'Thoughts on action learning' *Industrial and Commercial Training* Vol 15 No 1 January pp12-15

Consultancy

ARGYRIS, C 1961 'Explorations in consulting-client relationships' *Human Organisation* Vol 20 No 3 pp121-133. Reprinted in W Bennis, K Benne & R Chin (eds) 1970 *The planning of change* 2nd ed. London: Holt, Rinehart and Winston
Argyris argues that consultancy can only be effective if both consultant and client behave authentically, i.e. in accordance with their own values. He analyses two case studies to illustrate the problems that can arise if the consultant abandons his own values and uses the values of the client-system.

BEVAN, G 1981 'Croyland' in E Henderson and G Perry (eds) *Change and development in schools* Maidenhead: McGraw Hill
In this case study of a primary school's adaptation to open-plan accommodation other headteachers and Her Majesty's Inspectors acted as consultants.

BLAKE, R & MOUTON, J 1976 *Consultation* London: Addison-Wesley

BLAKE, R & MOUTON J 1976 'Strategies of consultation' in W Bennis, K Benne & R Chin (eds) *The planning of change* 3rd ed NY: Holt Rinehart and Winston

BOUD, D & McDONALD, R 1981 *Educational development through consultancy* Guildford: University of Surrey, Society for Research into Higher Education
A report on the use of consultancy to improve teaching in the tertiary sector of education. As such it does not address itself directly to the questions of support for educational management. However it does offer some useful advice on the process of consulting which has been found appropriate in education. The report covers questions of making initial contact, defining relevancy, methods of working and problems of reporting. Among

the models described is the "colleagual" model involving the collaboration of peers.

BOYDELL, T & PEDLER, M (eds) 1981 *Management self-development: concepts and practices* Farnborough: Gower pp223-239

BUCKLEY, J 1985 'Some issues of training methodology' in *The training of secondary school heads in Western Europe* Windsor: NFER-Nelson
Draws lessons for trainers from some of the experiences of various countries, with brief mention of the role of consultants.

BUCKLEY, J 1985 'How training needs are being met : Norway' in *The training of secondary school heads in Western Europe* Windsor: NFER-Nelson
The Hordaland B course – part of the national AMS training programme for school heads – includes the use of external consultants. The follow-up SIK (Schools in Contact) programme also involves support from outside agencies, including consultants.

COUNCIL OF EUROPE: COUNCIL FOR CULTURAL COOPERATION 1983 'Summary of discussion groups' findings' in *School management training in Europe* Report of the 12th Council of Europe Teachers' Seminar 21-26 September 1981 Donaueschingen. Strasbourg: Council of Europe
Summarises the conclusions of the discussion groups on various issues, including the issue of support from the inspectorate.

DEAN, J 1981 'Advisory service' in E Henderson and G Perry (eds) *Change and development in schools* Maidenhead: McGraw Hill
Describes the Surrey school-focused management training course for heads, which involved the author in a consultancy role. She spent a whole day at each head's school to provide her with a basis for planning discussions with the head, and visited each school every summer term (together with other inspectors) to follow up the implementation of the programme of development undertaken during the course, and to develop new plans.

ERAUT, M 1977 'Some perspectives on consultancy in in-service education' *British Journal of Inservice Education* Vol 4 No 1 & 2 pp95-99
Offers a preliminary typology of the consultant's roles, viz: expert; resource provider; promoter; career agent; link agent; inspector/evaluator; legitimator; ideas man; process helper; counsellor; and

change agent. The paper concludes by stressing two aspects affecting a consultant's credibility which particularly call for further research: 1) the power and authority gap between teachers and providers, and 2) the gap between the epistemological world of the teacher and the consultant.

EVERARD, K 1982 *Management in comprehensive schools – what can be learned from industry?* York: University of York, Centre for the Study of Comprehensive Schools
In this review of management training techniques used in industry which would be relevant to school management training Everard includes guidance on the selection of consultancy services.

FERGUSON, C 1970 'Concerning the nature of human systems and the consultant's role' in W Bennis, K. Benne and R. Chin (eds) 1970 *The planning of change* 2nd ed London: Holt Rinehart and Winston pp407-412 Reprinted from the *Journal of Applied Behavioural Science*
After a general analysis of the nature of human systems, Ferguson identifies the role of the consultant as explicator of the "non fit" between interfaces, releaser of forces that move towards balance or health in a human system, and precipitator of a process the substance of which comes from the members. He lists 17 activities the consultant can do: capture data; scan for troubled interfaces; promote psychological bonding; be a linking agent between people and/or groups; serve as communications conveyor; suspend animation and analyse process; assist in diagnostic formulation and reformulation of issues; lift up relationship problems and feeling data for consideration; use clinical skills to help make communication more congruent (effective); encourage feedback; serve as a plumber and/or obstetrician; promote spirit of enquiry; analyse ongoing problem-solving meetings; set up opportunities for mutual coaching and team-building; assist in the management of conflict; help promote a proper psychological climate; and take calculated risks because he is expendable.

HAVELOCK, R 1973 *The change agent's guide to innovation in education* New Jersey: Educational Technology Publications
Havelock's work on change agents and the process of innovation in education has perhaps had the widest circulation amongst educationalists in Britain over the last 15 years. The case studies and detailed prescription of the change agent's role are still a useful source of good practical advice for anyone wishing to work on a one

to one basis in support of a head.

KLEIN, D 1966 'Some notes on the dynamics of resistance to change: the defender role' in W Bennis, K Benne and R Chin (eds) 1970 *The planning of change* 2nd ed London: Holt Rinehart and Winston pp498-507
Argues that resistance to change is not necessarily negative, and that change agents should consider the possibility that defenders have something of great value to communicate about the nature of the system which the change agent is seeking to influence, and that the defender's participation in the change process may lead to the development of more adequate plans and the avoidance of hitherto unforeseen consequences. This thesis is of manifest relevance to consultants.

LIPPITT, G & R 1978 *The consulting process in action* La Jolla: University Associates

LIPPITT, R WATSON, J & WESTLEY, B 1958 *Planned change* New York: Harcourt Brace Jovanovitch

MORANT, R W 1981 *In-service education within the school* London: Allen and Unwin
Three pages (100-103) discuss the notion of consultancy, arguing that there are two basic consultancy roles: 1) process consultancy, concerned with means rather than ends, where the consultant is brought in at the beginning and offers guidance and analysis rather than imposing remedies and 2) the expert, called in after the teacher has articulated his needs.

MULFORD, B 1982 'Consulting with education systems is about the facilitation of coordinated effort' in H. Gray (ed) *The management of educational institutions: theory, research and consultancy* Lewes: Falmer Press
Writing from his experience and researches in OD, Mulford discusses the problem of the consultant.

OLSEN, E & OSEN, G 1981 'The use of external consultants for school development: a Norwegian case study' *School Organisation* Vol 1 No 1 pp11-19

SCHEIN, E 1969 *Process consultation: its role in organisational development* NY: Addison-Wesley
Offers a detailed account of the role which the process consultant can play both in interpersonal and in group events within a programme of organisation development. This extension of the

consultant's role into working with groups may be of particular interest in the context of the school.

SCHMUCK, R 1978 'Peer consultation for school improvement' in C Cooper and C Alderfer (eds) *Advances in experiential social processes Vol 1* Chichester: Wiley
Argues that peer consultation is an effective alternative to the traditional hierarchical professional-client helping relationship. Based on the experience of establishing two peer cadres of OD specialists to support school improvement (in Kent, Washington and Eugene, Oregon) Schmuck categorises the activities carried out by the cadres, the distinctive values embodied in the collegial relationships between the cadre members and clients, and the typical client groups. He concludes by giving advice on establishing and institutionalising OD peer cadres.

STEELE, F 1975 *Consulting for organisational change* Amherst: Univ. of Massachusetts Press

STUART, R 1984 'Maximising managers' day-to-day learning: frameworks for the practice of learning interventions' in C Cox and J Beck (eds) *Management development: advances in practice and theory* Chichester: Wiley
Provides frameworks to help the 'learning consultant' to understand the nature of individuals' learning problems and to identify appropriate interventions to reduce these problems. See under self-development.

The LEA Task Group

AJIMAL, K 1985 'Force field analysis: a framework for strategic thinking' *Long Range Planning* Vol 18 No 5 pp55-60
Illustrates the use and potential benefits of the Force Field Analysis technique for group problem-solving processes. Productivity groups or task forces working with a clear understanding of the force fields surrounding specific corporate problems are better placed to investigate, analyse and rectify problem areas.

ALEXANDER, L 1985 'Successfully implementing strategic decisions' *Long Range Planning* Vol 18 No 3 pp91-7
By means of a questionnaire to 93 US company residents, 10 common strategy implementation problems and 5 factors which help promote successful implementation were identified. Useful bibliography.

ANTHONY, R 1965 *Planning and control systems: a framework for analysis* Boston: Harvard University
A 20-year old book which might easily be set aside in favour of more recent publications. However it presents a short but readable review of some of the major issues and dilemmas covered in strategic planning, management and operational control. Provides a good background for anyone organising their task group with these kinds of intentions.

DAVIES, A 1981 'Strategic planning in the Thomas Cook Group' *Long Range Planning* Vol 14 No 5 pp27-38
Describes the annual planning cycle of Thomas Cook. The development of strategy takes place through various bodies – the Group Strategic Conference at Board level, the Group Planning Conference attended by operating company managers, and regional conferences in many of the territories. Models of the stages of the systematic planning process are provided.

EASTERBY-SMITH, M & DAVIES, J 1983 'Developing strategic thinking' *Long Range Planning* Vol 16 No 4 pp39-48
Having established that there is a need for managers to develop strategic thinking, the authors suggest a number of formal and informal techniques for developing the skills of strategic thinking – especially those involving taking advantage of the 'natural learning' that takes place on the job – and developing junior managers through projects and task forces.

EVERED, R 1983 'So what is strategy?' *Long Range Planning* June Vol 16 No 3 pp57-72
Compares the concept of strategy as it has developed in business management, military practice and futures research, identifying common and unique features. Concludes that corporate strategy is a mix of military and futures strategy and suggests options open to corporate strategists – like, for instance, doing nothing: 'unhappy the general ... with a system' (Napoleon).

HAWKINS, K & TARR, R 1980 'Corporate planning in local government: a case study' *Long Range Planning* Vol 13 No 2 pp43-51
A case study of corporate planning, describing how Bradford developed a three year corporate plan.

HREBINIAK, L & JOYCE, W 1984 *Implementing strategy* London: Collier Macmillan

A very detailed practical review of formulation and implementation of strategy. May be considered over-detailed in its approach but raises many interesting dimensions of analysis.

JOHNSON, G & SCHOLES, K 1984 *Exploring corporate strategy* London: Prentice Hall
Has useful sections on strategic decision making and analysis written in a straightforward, practical way and illustrated by short case studies. Understandably the main focus is on strategies in industry and commerce, but the main principles are clearly of relevance to education.

PETERS, T & WATERMAN, R 1983 'Beyond rational decision-making' *The McKinsey Quarterly* Spring pp19-30
Criticises over-reliance on analytical management techniques, suggesting that a preoccupation with rational decision-making can lead to concentration on cost reduction (rather than revenue enhancement), a distrust of experimentation, negative thinking, over-complexity/inflexibility, and a lack of internal competition. Calls for path finding and the idiosyncratic arts of implementation.

SIMS, D & EDEN, C 1984 'Futures research – working with management teams' *Long Range Planning* Vol 17 No 4 pp51-59
Case study of the use of looking at the future as a 'conscious dream' – represented as explicit models. Three housing managers in a local authority housing department used the method to articulate their own images of the future and to understand each other's images.

SKIPTON, M 1985 'Helping managers to develop strategies' *Long Range Planning* Vol 18 No 2 pp56-68
Offers a normative, procedural framework for strategic analysis and planning.

TENDAM, H 1984 'Strategic management in a firm of consulting engineers' *Long Range Planning* Vol 17 No 4 pp21-24
A case study of the introduction of strategic management in a large and diversified company of consulting engineers in Brazil. Project management was a successful joint venture between some top people inside and some external consultants, strongly interacting with each other, which resulted in plans and discussions. The article evaluates the success factors.